THE PARADOX OF PORN

Notes on Gay Male Sexual Culture

DON SHEWEY

Joybody Books • New York

The Paradox of Porn:
Notes on gay male sexual culture

Joybody Books • New York

Copyright 2018 by Don Shewey
All rights reserved.
Printed in the United States of America.

The Tom of Finland image in chapter 3 is used by permission. © 2018 Tom of Finland Foundation / Artists Rights Society (ARS), New York

No part of this book may be reproduced or transmitted in any form or by any means, electronic or mechanical, including photocopying, recording, or by any information storage and retrieval system, without permission in writing from the publisher. For information address: Joybody Books, 50 W. 56th Street, Suite 3A, New York, NY 10019-3856.

Cover design: Chip Kidd
Book design: Todd Cooper, All-D

Library of Congress Cataloguing-in-Publication Data is available upon request.

ISBN-13: 978-1-7321344-0-9 (paperback)
ISBN-13: 978-1-7321344-1-6 (e-book)

To Andy

TABLE OF CONTENTS

1.	Overview	7
2.	Rose and Thorn	13
3.	Timeline	21
4.	The Paradox of Porn	31
5.	Porn and Gay Male Sexual Norms	41
6.	Porn as Sex Education	47
7.	Your Brain on Porn	55
8.	Hitting the Pause Button	65
9.	Porn as Imagination Education	71
10.	Porn and Body Standards	79
11.	Size	87
12.	Virtual Sex vs. Real Sex	97
13.	Porn as Etiquette Instruction	105
14.	Wild Sex	111
15.	Personal History of Porn	121
16.	Porn as Life Force	131
17.	Porn as Comic Entertainment	137
18.	Porn as Gateway to Self-Knowledge	141
19.	Evolution of Hookup Culture	145
20.	Squirting	149
21.	Fucking	165
22.	Bottoming	171
23.	Daddy/Boy: Lover, Power, and Masculinity	181
24.	The Gift of Desire	187
25.	Conclusion	195
Appendix:	Use of Porn Study *(or, Don't Take My Word For It)*	203

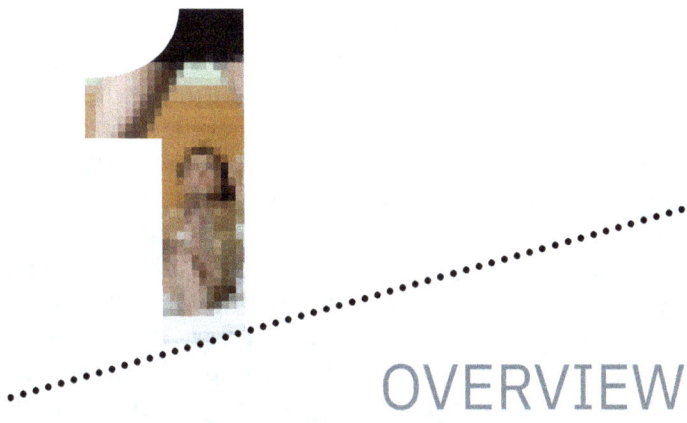

1 OVERVIEW

At the Rowe Labor Day retreat in Massachusetts for gay, bisexual, and questioning men in 2013, I conducted a workshop called "Learning from Porn." I felt ever-so-slightly scandalous broaching this topic while attending a conference at a Unitarian Universalist retreat center. At the same time, like my teacher and mentor Joseph Kramer, I'm committed to healing the split between sexuality and spirituality in our culture. We all have bodies, and it is our spiritual invitation to inhabit them completely and mindfully. Reading a poster in the Rowe library enumerating the core values of Unitarian Universalism, I resonated with its championing "a free and responsible search for truth and meaning."

As several workshop participants immediately acknowledged, we all have some kind of love/hate relationship with pornography. This ubiquitous entertainment heavily influences the norms by which we judge our bodies, our desires, and our sexual partners. But we hardly ever talk about it to anyone.

Most public discussions about pornography tend to focus on addiction, abuse, exploitation of women, and so on. We nod our heads in solemn agreement — yes, yes, those problems clearly exist — and then go back to consuming in private whatever pornography turns us on. There are very few forums where it's possible to have an open discussion about pornography without having to choose between condemnation and defensiveness. I believe that as human beings we always have a positive reason for doing what we do. As a middle-aged gay white sex therapist in New York City, especially one who works with a lot of gay men, I'm acutely aware of the paradox of porn – that however much it contributes to shame, compulsiveness, and distorted ideas about sexuality, looking at pornography is for many men an important doorway into erotic existence. I wanted to create a safe, non-judgmental context in which to consider a few pertinent questions: What is hot about porn? What myths about sex does porn perpetuate, for better or for worse? What aspects of pleasurable sexuality never show up in porn? I quickly learned that men have plenty to say on all these topics.

Anyone who is heterosexual grows up with abundant role models for courtship, dating, sexual exploration, partnering, parenting, even dealing with conflict and loss. We live in families that model all that for us, however imperfectly, and mainstream culture leaves no corner of heterosexual romance unexamined. For gay men, pornography provides not only entertainment and excitement but crucial exposure to same-sex attraction, unapologetic desire, uninhibited behavior, and fertile fantasy life – what is possible, what it looks like. Throughout decades when gay public life meant constantly battling ignorance and prejudice, physical danger and the terrible wrath of AIDS, pornography kept a secret channel open. By its very existence porn champions embodiment and erotic vitality in the face of sexual repression, political disenfranchisement, and religious pressure to deny the pleasures of the body.

"Pornography is the return of the repressed, of feelings and fantasies driven underground by a culture that atomizes sexuality, defines love as a noble affair of the heart and mind, lust as a base animal urge centered in unmentionable organs," wrote *Village Voice* columnist Ellen Willis, consistently one of the smartest thinkers on this subject among American intellectual commentators. "Prurience — the state of mind I associate with pornography — implies a sense of sex as forbidden, secretive pleasure, isolated from any emotional or social context. I imagine that in utopia, porn would wither away along with the state, heroin, and Coca-Cola. But for now the sexual impulses that pornography appeals to are part of virtually everyone's psychology."

Of course, as a curriculum for adult sex education, pornography is woefully incomplete. Yet we often consciously or unconsciously accept gay male porn as if it's an instruction manual, mistaking its formulaic narratives for documentary filmmaking.

At Rowe, I asked my guys to identify some of the myths that porn perpetuates about male sexuality. Here are some that got mentioned: Dicks are always huge and always hard. Sex always leads to fucking, with limited foreplay or preliminaries. Everyone can fuck and get fucked. Everyone squirts gallons of jizz. Everyone is great looking, perfectly groomed, buff, and tattooed. Sex is instantaneous – as soon as you want it, you can have it, and you cut right to the chase. There's no expression of emotion, no setting of boundaries, and no talking or negotiating about HIV status or using condoms. Everything works, and sex is easy.

We talked about the distorted notions that arise as a consequence of steeping yourself in the world of porn. In porn, sex happens magically, but in real life making a connection is much more confusing and complicated. The gap between how easy it looks online and how difficult it is offline exacerbates social anxiety. The digital devices on which many of us have grown increasingly dependent can wreak havoc for people with addictive/compulsive tendencies. Porn promotes extreme objectification and unrealistic standards of male anatomy and performance. All emotions are sexualized. Pornography can take over your erotic imagination so completely that you equate sex with porn, and it becomes easy to forget that you don't have to be sitting in front of a computer or fondling a smartphone to have sex.

Independent feature films have gotten better at capturing the nuances of emotional intimacy between men. I'm thinking especially about recent films such as Andrew Haigh's *Weekend*, Ira Sachs's *Keep the Lights On*, John Cameron Mitchell's *Shortbus*, and Travis Mathews's *I Want Your Love*. But if the only gay films you watch are porn, you don't get a chance to observe difficult conversations, make-up sex after a fight, changing the bedsheets when buttsex gets messy, or virtually anything about emotional or romantic life beyond sex.

Still, regardless of the negative consequences, many if not most gay men spend time on a regular basis looking at and/or jacking off to porn. Some porn stars and producers (name your favorite) have become as essential to gay culture as the female divas of stage, screen, and song. But tastes are highly individual. We don't all look at the same porn. What constitutes "porn" has morphed generation by generation from the underwear pages of the Sears & Roebuck catalog to physique magazines to pulpy paperbacks to glossy monthlies. Dirty movies and boothstores gave way to the home video revolution. The internet paved the way for chat rooms, online porn, streaming video, social media, GPS-based hookup sites, smartphone apps, Tumblr blogs, and whatever just got invented last week.

For me, the best thing about the session at Rowe was witnessing the powerful questions that the men in attendance asked themselves as a result of participating in an open and honest community discussion about how pornography affects our lives. What have I learned about myself, my desires, and my fantasies from porn? How has it expanded my vision of what sex between men can be? How do I use porn as validation? How does porn train me to treat real men like objects? How do I use porn as a barrier to intimacy, as a substitute for contact? How is porn a gateway to addiction for me? How does it perpetuate unhealthy compartmentalization in my life? How does it lull me into thinking everybody has to identify as either a top or a bottom? How does it keep me stuck in my shame?

These are questions I've spent a lot of time thinking about. I've struggled with them in my private life, and they show up in my professional life on a daily basis. The theories, ideas, and observations I explore in this piece of writing come from a combination of personal experience, broad reading, teaching workshops, and being in private practice for twenty years with the gay, straight, bisexual, transgender, questioning, and undeclared people who come to me for psychotherapy, sex therapy, erotic mentoring, intimacy coaching, couples counseling, sex education, erotic bodywork, and sacred intimacy. (Bear in mind that when I share stories from sessions with clients, all names and identifying details have been changed to preserve confidentiality.)

This is not, by any means, a scholarly treatise but an informed, opinionated, open-ended, sometimes extremely graphic meditation on the topic of pornography and its impact on gay male sexual culture. I have not undertaken a comprehensive history of pornography. I don't pretend to speak knowledgeably about heterosexual porn. The moral, ethical, and legal issues surrounding sexual imagery depicting children are a separate matter altogether and will not be addressed here.

I'm offering not a seamless narrative but a kind of postmodern critical essay indebted to Susan Sontag and Roland Barthes, whose work exemplified the power of thinking out loud in assembled fragments. I'm also very specifically inspired by Eric Rofes' *Dry Bones Breathe*, Samuel Delany's *The Motion of Light in Water*, and Paul B. Preciado's *Testo Junkie*, which model the freedom to weave intensely personal experience and sociopolitical commentary into theoretical writing. This book comprises extended riffs on a variety of themes from different angles in multiple voices, attempting to unpack the complexity and contradiction of my subject in plain language, without academic jargon. Not everyone thinks the way I do. Feel free to argue with me. This is my opinion. Call it my sermon on a subject too large and charged for anyone to have the last word on.

I'm all for waking up to the joy of life in a body. Pornography can contribute to the joy of physical pleasure and emotional connection, and it can also turn into an obstacle. I'm writing in the hopes of continuing this conversation to make space for awareness of both possibilities.

2

ROSE AND THORN

My ex-boyfriend Harvey Redding is an artist and illustrator. One of the first presents he ever gave me was a copy of an illustration he drew for one of the slick porn magazines, *Honcho* or *Inches*. In the picture, a prisoner crouches naked at the feet of a correctional officer in thigh-high boots, seen from the waist down. They both have huge erections. Underneath the picture, Harvey hand-wrote a loving inscription that cemented our bond. It said, "Suck my big dick you filthy scumbag." I immediately taped this treasure over my desk. It turned me on and it made me laugh.

Here are some things I love about gay-male porn:
1. Unlike all the movies and TV shows I watched when I was growing up, pornography depicts a world where everyone is enthusiastically, unapologetically gay. When I came out into a full-blown gay community, as part of the first post-Stonewall generation, that was the most basic, innocent, and liberating aspect of gay porn.

Suck my big dick you gilthy scumbag ——!

2. I love the fact that everyone is sexually available. No matter what they look like or what their occupation is, any character that shows up in pornography — whether poolboy or postman or airline pilot — will end up sucking or getting sucked, fucking or getting fucked. That's automatically attractive to me. I have little patience with the hard-to-get.
3. In gay porn, most people enjoy having sex.
4. They show everything, every inch of their bodies and every imaginable sex act. In doing so, they defy encrusted psychosocial inhibitions. In *The Ego and the Mechanisms of Defense*, Anna Freud wrote,

> *There is in human nature a disposition to*

> *repudiate certain instincts, in particular the sexual instincts, indiscriminately and independently of individual experience. This disposition appears to be a phylogenetic inheritance, a kind of deposit accumulated from acts of repression practiced by many generations, and merely continued, not initiated, by individuals.*

I think I know exactly what she means. No matter how much we love and enjoy sex and naked bodies, looking at them and licking them and inhabiting them — in other words, no matter what a slutty sacred sex-pig I am — still when we see depictions of sex something inside of us goes, "That's bad! That's wrong!" One night years ago I was flipping through the cable TV stations in New York and landed on an excerpt of a William Higgins screen test in which a bland blond Southern California boy stripped naked and perched on a bed with his butt in the air while the director's assistant efficiently and matter-of-factly shaved the hair around his butthole. Part of me thought, "They shouldn't be showing this on TV." That's the "phylogenetic inheritance" Anna Freud talks about. Another part of me was absolutely riveted. I love how pornography categorically and systematically rejects mindless obedience to generations of sexual repression. "That's so bad! That's so wrong! That's so hot!"

5. Most hetero porn I've witnessed buys into patriarchal and sexist dynamics lock-stock-and-barrel. Gay porn models a sexual egalitarianism that I prize. Even when scenes pivot on power struggles, the power dynamic is usually fluid and flexible. I still remember

my amazement and then joy watching a classic old-school porn film called *Hothouse* when the studly star Jack Wrangler, whose humongous dick was usually the object of other guys' ministrations, leaned over and went down on someone else, thereby demolishing the myth that hot well-hung tops can only be serviced and never reciprocate.

6. In his book *The Re-Enchantment of Everyday Life*, Thomas Moore talks about pornography as a contemporary representation of religious traditions in which certain days are set aside for complete release from all sexual inhibitions and loyalties.

> *Over half the American population, according to some studies, engage in extramarital sex, and so one is tempted to conclude that something in the most dedicated people desires sex outside marriage ... Pornography often shows a similar interest in group sex, so that sexually explicit magazines echo certain ancient religious practices, and pornography casts its spell as carnival too, a release from the constraints of civilized mores.*

I always like reasonable-sounding arguments that connect sex with spiritual practice. When I register the ubiquity of porn images in gay male photocollage art, I tend to see it as related to religious kitsch. In Catholic society or in Hindu society, you see images of deities everywhere, unquestioned, often in ridiculous manifestations (think of those "3-D" lenticular postcards of Christ on the cross). That's what pictures of naked men are to queers — objects of worship, almost indiscriminately worshipped. But I prefer Moore's analysis of porn images as "spell-binding" rather than simply kitschy. In addition to "Suck my big dick you filthy scumbag," I've kept on my bulletin board other pornographic images — another drawing by Harvey of a crewcut guy on his back with his legs in the air (V for Victory) displaying his star-like butthole, and a color picture from a magazine of a rather blank-faced hunk sporting an impressive boner — that have on numerous occasions helped re-energize me (re-enchant me) when I'm stuck on some writing problem.

7. I like that porn gives me new ideas about sex practices beyond my usual patterns. For instance, as a baby fag I was revolted by the very idea of rimming. Lick where someone poops? Ugh! No way! Then I saw a porn film in which a handsome mustachioed performer so lovingly and passionately applied his lips to another guy's butthole that I suddenly made the connection to kissing. Now it's practically my favorite expression of intimacy. Time and time again, porn has spurred me to recognize and embrace what really turns me on. A hard dick doesn't lie. Reading stylized stories about daddy-boy scenes made me realize how much that dynamic is a part of my erotic imagination. I guess I've learned a lot about myself from my response to taboo stuff like violence, coercion, and masochism. It disturbs me to admit how much rape scenes turn me on, for instance. (The male rape scene in the basement of the pawnshop in *Pulp Fiction* comes to mind, as does the gruesome hotel-room gang-bang in *Leaving Las Vegas*.) Just the opposite of Andrea Dworkin and Catherine McKinnon's assertions, I believe that gay porn has taught me I don't have to act

on these desires/impulses. I'm glad to know I have violent sexual fantasies, and I believe the knowledge means I'm less likely to act them out unconsciously, as either perpetrator or victim.

Here are some things I don't love about gay male porn:

1. I don't love the alienated, heartless culture that has grown up around gay porn — the peep shows, the video booths, the phone lines, the personal ads, the hook-up websites, the smartphone apps — where we reduce each other to body parts and physical descriptions. Or insatiable disembodied eyeballs. "There's no surer way to kill the action in a cruise bar than to put porn on a big screen," says my friend Wayne Hoffman. "Suddenly, a bar that used to be packed with men looking at each other, having sex in the back or taking each other home turns into a theater with everyone standing still, silently facing front, watching a big screen, avoiding eye contact and body contact with other patrons, before going home alone, horny." This disconnectedness sometimes mirrors the attitude portrayed in porn itself, which leads me to …

2. I don't love porn as a guideline for real sexual encounters. In porn the people barely say two words to one another before falling into the most intimate sexual encounters. In my experience that's rarely a recipe for satisfying sex. For one thing, if you're trying to have sex without spreading diseases, some negotiation around levels of protection is a good idea. It's not just a medical consideration, though. We need to talk to each other about what we like

and don't like, what we want and don't want in sexual encounters. Porn models silence in the place of speaking desire, which can be soul-deadening.
3. Just as bad as silence is the macho grunting that passes for verbal communication in porn films. In films, it can be stylized, and it's laughable. When the same ridiculously minimal poverty-stricken dialogue (my friend Dave succinctly describes it as "[Verb] that [noun]!") shows up in the bedroom or in the midst of some otherwise torrid sexual encounter, it makes my heart sink.
4. Let's face it, porn has had a bad influence on gay male sexual etiquette. One of my pet peeves is the lack of after-care in our sexual encounters. In porn, once the guys shoot their creamy loads, the scene is basically over — we almost never see any cuddling, any wiping up, any showering, any making tea, any falling asleep in each other's arms, any sharing of snacks. So in life, at the baths or any place guys congregate for sex these days, cum-and-go is the name of the game. I've had encounters where literally, less than 60 seconds after squirting, the guy is out the door, and I'm left thinking: what was that all about?
5. I really don't love the privileging of certain body types in gay male porn. There's not nearly enough variety for my taste. A huge percentage of porn features either smooth blond hairless/shaved skinny boys aged 20-24 or hairless tattooed muscle guys. Look around you. How many people do you know who look like that? It pains me to meet otherwise intelligent grown men who have developed severe body shame

because they don't look like the guys in porn films and magazines. My selfish reason for disliking this aspect of gay porn is that I'm not AT ALL turned on by those skinny blond boys or tattooed muscle studs. I've always had a thing for older guys with male-pattern baldness, salt-and-pepper hair, a slight paunch. Happily, the internet era has evolved countervailing trends to accommodate all tastes: old-guy porn, fat-guy porn, little-dick porn, hairy-guy porn. That's why I often prefer written porn to visual porn — that way I can eternally be the idealistic young man looking for love from the big hairy gruff but loving daddy of my dreams.

As a consumer of gay male porn, I'm pretty easily satisfied. Harvey's drawing showed it doesn't take much to get me going. I don't need porn to match my reality, or to live up to my utopian political expectations, or to solve my self-esteem problems, or anybody else's. Porn has nothing to prove to me. The best thing it can do is unleash my passionate desire to live one more day — to suck dick like the filthy scumbag I am. Is that too much to ask?

3

TIMELINE

> *"If we invent a machine, the first thing we are going to do – after making a profit – is use it to watch porn."*
> —Damon Brown,
> *Computer Games Magazine*, 2006

Let's consider the history of how we watch porn. Since human beings first started creating images, sex has been a popular subject to represent. Not that sexual imagery has always been viewed as pornographic. That term has a very specific historical derivation. "Pornography is the inheritance of Victorian conceptualizations," says University of Cambridge art historian Simon Goldhill in *Pornography: the secret history of civilization*, a six-part series for British television. "We'd like to think that pornography is natural. It's not natural. It's a modern cultural invention." Scholars note the powerful impact on Victorian society of the unearthing in Pompeii of ruins that included an astonishing array of art works reflecting the place of sexual imagery in ancient Roman culture.

"In the mid-18th century an Italian peasant stumbled upon the remains of the ancient city of Pompeii, buried by the eruption of Mt. Vesuvius, nearly 17 centuries earlier," the documentary explains. "As excavators dug, they revealed an untouched record of ancient Roman life. The frozen city immediately gripped the public imagination. But as the excavators uncovered more of this petrified town, they experienced the first tremors of unease. As each new villa was revealed, this unease turned to anxiety and anxiety to panic. The noble ancient world they were exposing was one which, in their eyes, was contaminated at every turn by the obscene. Among the first objects they unearthed was a marble statue. It depicted the Roman god Pan in explicit sexual intercourse with a goat, provoking both horror and fascination. The excavators' panicked response to this image began a process which would culminate in the legal prohibition of explicit sexual material which today we would describe as pornography."

In ancient Rome sex was viewed as a normal part of life, and erotic artwork conveyed a sense of life's pleasures. Scholars tell us that Romans believed that pictures never hurt anyone. Sexual behavior was socially regulated and governed by self-control, quite separate from artistic representation. Pictures of taboo, intimate, sexual acts created outrageous laughter by breaking the rules of public comportment. Images of Hermes or Priapus with an erect phallus belonged at the front door as protection against evil spirits. The gods were fucking all the time, polyamorous and pansexual. The discoveries at Pompeii suggest that those artworks were created to give people permission to be enjoy the sight of naked sexual bodies.

Yet when these same images surfaced in the Victorian era, an entirely different mindset greeted sexual imagery. It was felt that these explicit pictures would cause viewers – male viewers, of course (it would be unthinkable for Victorian women to be exposed to such material) – to become "disturbed" (i.e., aroused), which would lead to masturbation, a guilty pleasure to which they would become addicted. And in a sense, that Victorian fear came true! But since you can't regulate internal feelings of arousal or prurience, the Victorians decided that it was the sexual images themselves that created harm and set about devising legislation to regulate their public availability. We have a lot of life force stuffed in the genie's bottle, and it comes out as porn.

Shards of pottery from ancient Greece on display in the finest museums all over the world show cheerful sexual frolics and line drawings of muscular athletes with contemporary comments (καλός, meaning "beautiful" or "hot"). Not long after the printing press was invented, books of sexy stories and erotic drawings started getting published. The earliest form of photography came about in 1839; seven years later, the first pornographic daguerreotype that we know about appeared (although the word "pornography" didn't officially enter the English language until 1857). Ditto with film. The first commercially available film appeared in 1896, and by 1915 a thriving industry circulated crude "stag films," illegally shot, distributed through an underground network, and viewed primarily by private all-male gatherings. Sex researcher Alfred Kinsey avidly collected and even produced "stag films," sometimes with the assistance of gay writer and pornographer Samuel Steward (the subject of Justin Spring's illuminating biography *The Secret Historian*). Tame as it may seem now, Playboy started a revolution

Greek bowl (detail), 5th century BC

in American sexual culture when 27-year-old Hugh Hefner decided to publish a mainstream magazine devoted to pictures of naked women in 1953.

Magazines figure prominently in the history of contemporary gay male pornography. The first homoerotica discreetly available on certain newsstands consisted of muscle magazines that didn't even pretend to offer advice to bodybuilders but filled its pages with studio portraits of beefcake models wearing little more than posing straps. The obscenity laws prohibiting frontal male nudity changed in 1968, which paved the way for periodicals featuring naked men starting in 1973 with *Playgirl*, which supposedly catered to newly liberated, sexually empowered women. The spreads of shirtless Broadway chorus boys in the closety show-biz monthly *After Dark* gave way to openly gay magazines like *In Touch* (launched

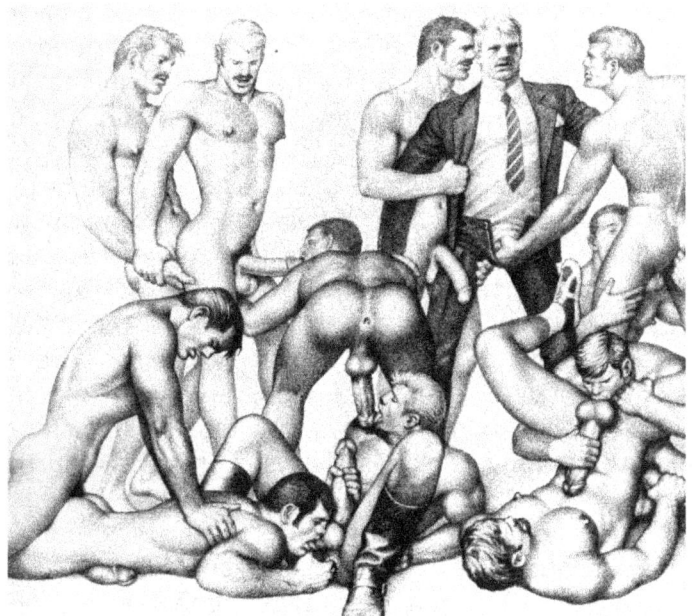

Tom of Finland drawing (detail), 1981

in 1974), *Blueboy* (1976), *Mandate* (1977), *Playguy*, and *Honcho* (both 1978).

Pornographic movies emerged from the underground in the 1970s. Straight fuck-flicks like *Behind the Green Door* and *Deep Throat* made a lot of money and spawned an industry of not only filmmakers and distributors but also movie theaters specializing in porn. The famous concentration of grindhouses on 42nd Street ("the Deuce") in New York City's Times Square inspired smaller-scaled "red-light" districts in other cities, and a subset of these cinemas devoted themselves to "all-male" films. The popular image of porn theaters and the related phenomenon of boothstores had them catering to businessmen sitting with their raincoats over their laps discreetly wanking. The gay moviehouses were more like de facto sex clubs with man-on-man action happening not only onscreen but in the balconies and back rows, which then got reflected in the content of porn classics like *Back Row* and *A Night at the Adonis* (shot at the famous, now-defunct gay movie palace on Eighth Avenue).

Home video killed the porno moviehouses but created overnight a vast audience for privately consumed pornography. JVC created the videocassette in 1976, and two years later, although only 1% of American households had videocassette recorders (VCRs), something like 75% of tapes sold were pornographic. "We may take it for granted now," wrote Carrie Weisman in an entertaining thumbnail history of pornography ("Sex has always been a story worth sharing") for the online newsmagazine AlterNet. "But the ability to pause, fast-forward, rewind, and rewatch video changes the experience entirely." DVDs emerged in 1995, and their higher quality buried the earlier generation of porn video. But then the World Wide Web made its debut in 1991. By 1995 ubiquitous internet access entered our lives, and as the song from the Broadway musical *Avenue Q* so bluntly put it, "The Internet Is For Porn." Starting in 2006, streaming video made the creation and distribution of commercial and amateur porn more available than ever.

The technology built specifically to facilitate cruising for sex partners has its own quaint history. In the 1960s and '70s, guys who were too closeted or too geographically isolated or not socially adept enough to meet people on the street or in bars would place discreet, often intricately coded advertisements in the "personals" sections in the back pages of certain newspapers. That was big business for New York's alternative weekly *The Village Voice*. *The Advocate*, the California-based national gay newsmagazine, had an entire special advertising supplement ("the pink pages") of personal ads in each issue. In the 1980s phone sex lines became another way to make safe, anonymous connections. In the early pre-internet days of personal computers, when giant clunky machines could only connect via dial-up modems, virtual "bulletin boards" were a way to leave messages, have conversations, and meet partners. When America Online (AOL) hit the scene in 1985, it didn't take long for chat rooms to gain popularity for chatting and hooking up (long before that expression came to mean "meeting for sex").

Of course, every development in the technology of cruising for sex made it incrementally easier not just to meet anonymous or pseudonymous partners but also to get obsessed with the hunt and addicted to checking checking checking. Craigslist began in 1995 with its free, no-frills listings popular with apartment hunters, people selling used furniture, and "Men Seeking Men." Both AOL's chat rooms and Craigslist's personals were organized by cities and sometimes neighborhoods, and they cast a wide net. As with phone sex lines, the ease of anonymous contact allowed guys of all sexual persuasions to explore man-on-man fantasies without having to commit to any overtly gay lifestyle. Inevitably, specifically gay forums arose for chatting and meeting for sex. Gay.com created a thriving network of chat rooms and personal ads as well as entertainment news and lifestyle features (PlanetOut). Connexion, a website created by gay philanthropist Tim Gill, was for several years (2003-2011) a popular site for gay news and social networking. Numerous websites built to facilitate dating came and went; one of the most popular and long-running is Match.com, which began in 1995. These websites allowed viewers to create profiles, post pictures, browse other people's info, and send and receive private messages.

Gaydar emerged in 1999, making no pretense of being anything other than a forum for online cruising. Other more successful websites followed: Recon, for kinky men (2000); Manhunt (2001); Gay Romeo (2002); Adam4Adam (2003); Daddyhunt (2005), for older guys and the men who love them (founded, incidentally, by Christopher Turner, the much-younger husband of Armistead Maupin). Once Apple introduced the iPhone in 2007, it was only a matter of time before GPS-driven smartphone apps for cruising showed up. Grindr wasn't necessarily first out of the gate but starting in 2009 it became the gold-standard for apps that can tell you who's available for sex right now within two blocks or two miles of your location. After that came Scruff (2010) and its rivals (Jack'd, GROWLr, etc.) and the mobile versions of Manhunt and other websites. Mobile apps and instant messaging had the same impact on gay cruising that the internet had on broadcast and print journalism — it created a relentless, insatiable 24/7 demand.

The experience of using mobile apps for cruising is different from watching porn in many ways. Theoretically, we use hookup apps in order to connect with another person for sex; porn is usually a solo adventure in voyeuristic sex without another person. Yet because we all walk around now with cameras in our pockets, the reality is that more than ever we are surrounded by homemade porn. We take pictures of our dicks and videos of our hookups and circulate them by text message, and we hoard sexy pix we've received or encountered online. And this is where the consequences of pornography show up big-time. Although theoretically amateur porn could be creative and highly individualized, much of the time it turns out to reproduce the stylized sexual norms you see in commercial porn, increasing the allure of Performing Like an X-Tube Porn Star.

The ease of hooking up offers the promise of more love, more erotic satisfaction, more connection, less loneliness. And sometimes the promise gets fulfilled. Nevertheless, mobile apps like Grindr – which "delivers sexualized torsos tiled in the no-space of a smartphone screen: bodies without spaces, pure grid and no mass, frictionless, smooth erotic pulses" (Max Fox, *Gay & Lesbian Review*) — also offer one more way for gay men to judge and reject each other, to treat each other coldly and cruelly, and to feel left out.

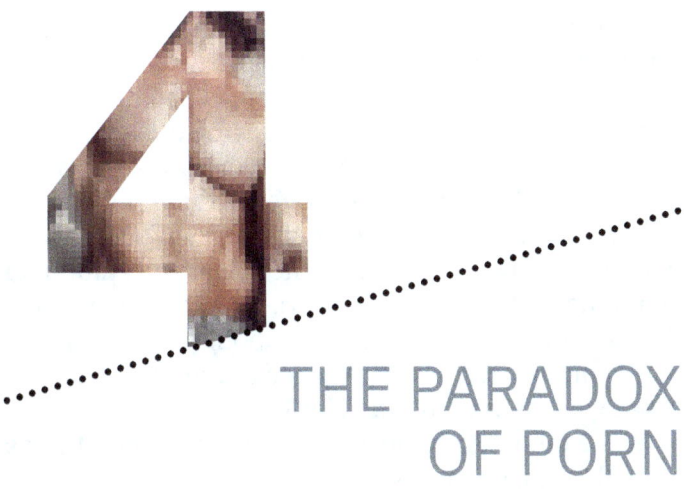

THE PARADOX OF PORN

Easy access to porn has had a huge impact on the sex lives of men. Starting with the advent of home video in the early 1980s and accelerating exponentially in the age of the internet and smartphones, porn has helped generations of men around the world to educate themselves about the spectrum of sexual possibilities, to explore their desires and their curiosities in private, to combat ignorance and shyness and shame and isolation, to pleasure themselves in periods when they are without partners, and to keep erotic awareness and expansion alive in the face of fears about disease, rejection, and body image. Certainly for gay men who came of age sexually in the mid-1980s, when the AIDS epidemic planted the equation that sex = death, beating off (with the assistance of porn or not) provided the easiest positive outlet for sexual pleasure that was certifiably free of risk for contracting a deadly disease. (Even mutual masturbation could trigger creative paranoia about getting infected by flying jizz.) That continues to be the case to the present day, even when fear of AIDS isn't necessarily central to most guys' thinking about sex.

Of course, like any other human phenomenon, pornography has its dark aspects as well. Although it vividly conveys certain kinds of information about sex, and it models many varieties of openness and acceptance of sexual desires, its version of adult sex education is far from ideal. It offers a distorted picture of what constitutes sex and what normal bodies look like, and it leaves out many of the social and emotional elements that make erotic interaction truly satisfying. If you get all your information about sex from porn, you're out of luck when it comes to the particulars of how to talk about anything, for instance.

The fallout from porn shows up in my practice as a sex therapist in many forms:

- guys who try to duplicate the extremely formulaic contortions of porn and find that it's not that enjoyable, and they think it's their problem;
- guys who think it's their job to perform like a porn star (get hard on cue, fuck like a jackhammer, and spurt without fail every time), or think that their partners expect them to do so, and therefore develop mild to crippling anxiety that interferes with their ability to function sexually;
- guys who are so accustomed to masturbating looking at porn that they find it difficult or impossible to climax in someone else's presence and/or to climax any way other than stroking themselves;
- guys who don't have much real-life experience with sex who are afraid even to date because they assume that any partner will expect them

to be ready to engage in every conceivable sex act (whether that's fucking or fisting); and
- guys who develop an addiction to looking at porn that interferes with the normal functioning of life.

Those aren't the only possible consequences of looking at porn, by any means, but those are some of the ways I have seen it become problematic for my clients.

* * *

Dean runs a lot of toxic stories about being uptight, inexperienced, and frigid. The reality is that he has had plenty of sex in his life, starting with an adolescent relationship with a neighborhood kid. After that, he didn't have sex in high school or college, dated a little in his twenties, and conducted a not-very-satisfying 15-year relationship. Most of his sexual energy has been channeled into masturbation, which he's done at least once daily most of his adult life, often using porn – first magazines, now internet porn. Inspired by seeing *The Sessions*, Ben Lewin's 2012 film based on Mark O'Brien's memoir as a man with cystic fibrosis who undertakes surrogate partner therapy, he asked his psychiatrist for a referral to a male sex surrogate. A web search came up empty. Dean went to an escort, had two sessions, and was able in the second one to ejaculate in someone else's presence for the first time in decades, possibly ever.

He came to me for help expanding his ability to enjoy sex. After an initial intake, I suggested we approach our second session with the intention for him to receive touch and pleasure with no agenda, no pressure for anything to happen. I gave him a thorough full-body massage including erotic touch, and perhaps unsurprisingly the first thing he said afterwards was, "Well, I didn't respond," meaning he didn't get a full erection. I thought that was precisely what we'd agreed not to expect, but perhaps I should have explicitly predicted that such self-conscious thinking would arise, as a prelude to setting it aside. I asked him how much of the time he was present for the experience and how much he was in his head expecting something else to happen. He said 50/50. That was even more presence than I would have guessed, so this was good information.

I noticed that, while being massaged, he barely breathed. He liked light touch. He liked everything I did around his anus. He was a little chilly at first so the warm oil I used and the hot towel I draped over him at the end were very appreciated. He enjoyed having his nipples touched. But apparently unless he has a raging hard-on, he doesn't really register penis pleasure. This gave me the useful information that his body does respond but his mind equates "responding" with "hard cock" and cancels out or disqualifies his many other forms of response. I realized that for someone like Dean, whose direct experiences of sex are vastly outnumbered by the amount of sex he has witnessed via pornography, there is a mistaken understanding of the natural/normal functions of touch and sexual arousal.

In gay porn you virtually never see a dick that isn't fully erect. What you never see onscreen in porn are the times when the performers lose their erections — they're simply edited out. Nor do you see the guys in porn injecting their penises with Caverject or Trimix, which is what guarantees that they sustain an erection in order to perform for the camera. So it's very easy to get the impression that all guys have hard cocks the entire time they're having sex. Whereas in real life, hardly anyone has an erection continuously from first touch to orgasm. Many guys need direct stimulation with a hand or a mouth for their dicks to get hard.

Dicks go up and down, up and down over the course of an encounter, and that becomes more pronounced with age.

You would never know that from just watching porn because the natural ebb-and-flow of erotic arousal isn't especially photogenic. Porn relies so heavily on a sustained pitch of hard-core action that the sight of a limp dick can be a turn-off; the viewer loses interest and moves on. And that attitude transfers to real-life encounters. Partners may well lose interest or blame themselves if someone's erection disappears. Many sexual encounters are driven by a medium-to-high level of anxiety about sustaining erections, lest that happen. It takes a certain amount of maturity and experience to trust that erections aren't the only indication of excitement and attraction. There's a lot of internal responsiveness going on when there's kissing, touching, and other simple forms of sensual body contact. Meanwhile, in porn you see a lot of highly active physical contact — punching, spitting, pissing, etc. — that may be diverting to watch in a movie but not always as pleasurable to experience in real life.

My suggestion for Dean was for him to experiment with cutting back on jerking off to porn — maybe not all at once, but little by little over time — and to increase his direct experience of intimate physical contact, and let the latter look like exactly what it looks like, without holding it up against the exciting but distorted examples of sex he sees in porn.

* * *

I believe porn is something that everyone has some kind of relationship with, whether openly or secretly, not unlike food, exercise, sleep, work, and intoxicants. All can be enjoyably used in moderation and harmful in excess, and it's up to each individual to determine what constitutes excess – easier said than done.

For many gay men, porn is inextricably bound up with sex and masturbation. Some guys can't masturbate without porn. Some guys can't go a day without masturbating. Some guys masturbate for pleasure, but lots of guys masturbate to relieve anxiety and to put themselves to sleep at night. And it's easy to get these things all jumbled up together.

Are there good ways to use porn? My perception is that it's pretty individual, and that everyone has a good way to use porn. The question is what percentage of our porn consumption leads to enjoyment rather than other outcomes. Is the experience of looking at porn enlivening, or is it deadening? Is it awakening, or is it anesthetizing? It's probably not all one or the other – what's the balance for you?

One of my teachers and colleagues, sex educator Joseph Kramer, has done a lot of masturbation coaching and has analyzed the way men use porn for self-pleasuring. For one thing, he notes how watching porn and having sex with another person are two entirely different experiences physiologically. Video porn floods the brain with fast-paced, highly edited stimulation that bombards the nervous system with many impressions per minute. Sex with a person is much slower, with neurons firing at a much reduced rate. His sound advice is to understand how different they are and not to expect sex with a person to provide the same kind of charge as looking at porn. He has also noticed how easy it is to become a disembodied robot looking at porn, so he counsels men to position themselves in relation to whatever screen they're viewing so their own penises are in the line of vision. Try it for yourself. See if it makes a difference.

One client I have worked with — Malcolm is married, bisexual, and in his 70s — has a very contained routine of looking at porn. Once a week he rents space at an internet cafe to look at gay porn (specifically pictures or video clips of men fucking and explicitly displaying their assholes) in order to stoke his imagination when he's making love with his wife, as he does once or twice a week. This sensible and practical approach to porn consumption nevertheless brings up deep pockets of guilt and shame about masturbation and sexual fantasies, clearly traceable to his religious upbringing, which taught that the only permissible receptacle for a man's seed is the vagina of his lawfully wedded wife.

I know couples who use porn to get themselves turned on before having sex with each other. I've frequently counseled couples to look at porn together — not in order to duplicate what they're watching but as a catalyst for talking about their fantasies, their curiosities, what they like and don't like. Those are intimate conversations that we don't have with just anyone. However, I must say that few couples actually take my suggestion. At first I couldn't understand the hesitation. What do established couples have to lose by sharing the contents of their erotic imaginations?

Then I stopped to consider how that works in my own relationship. My husband and I are for the most part very open to talking about sex, what we do, what we like, who and what turns us on. We're not sexually possessive; we know that we each have sexual tastes that the other may not be able to fulfill, and we're emotionally secure enough to give each other permission to explore to our hearts' content. We're both enthusiastic connoisseurs of pornography, yet it's not something we spend much time viewing together. I know that he has a robust personal relationship with porn. He belongs to the generational cohort for whom looking at and jerking off to porn was a godsend when he was an adolescent during the early and worst years of the AIDS epidemic. I'm always curious to know what he's looking at and a little surprised when he's shy about showing me. I have a general sense of what types of bodies and narratives he's drawn to. Does he worry that I will judge his choices? Does he think I'll be threatened by the amount of time he spends looking at porn and pleasuring himself? Does he fear that I will shame him for not reserving that erotic attention for me?

At the same time, I witness my own mixed feelings about sharing porn. He occasionally peeks over my shoulder when I'm scrolling through XXX pix on my Tumblr blog, and I like it when he does. But I realize there's a difference between that kind of casual glancing at porn, which is like idly shopping for clothes, and serious porn consumption, which is like setting out on a mission to buy a new pair of shoes. When I'm deeply engrossed in watching some daddy-boy sex scene or a marathon bareback gang-bang video, riveted to the screen, stroking myself, huffing poppers, and talking back to the participants, I'm in an exquisitely vulnerable state, both controlled and open. I'm at a sensitive threshold of erotic embodiment. I'm working to expand my erotic energy, not repress it. I'm engaging with porn as a tool for intimacy with myself, making love with my own fantasies, the porn providing access to some unusual depths of embodied desire. I don't necessarily want to be observed in this state because I don't want to be judged or evaluated. Nor do I want sensible, rational, left-brain consciousness to intrude on my erotic reverie. It's a deeply private moment, and all intimate relationships require a certain amount of privacy. Some couples maintain joint bank accounts and share e-mail addresses as easily as they wear each other's clothes, and that represents commitment. But it's equally reasonable that some couples achieve the same level of commitment through a balance of separateness and togetherness.

So when it comes to sharing porn, we do it indirectly, in the very 21st century form of following each other's Tumblr blogs. I'm delighted to see what he posts when it shows up on my Tumblr feed. And any time he wants to know what sweet/sexy/nasty porn has caught my eye, all he has to do is tune into mine.

Illustration by Josman

5
PORN AND GAY MALE SEXUAL NORMS

In order to do justice to the intricacy and complexity of the sexual issues that gay men wrestle with, I want to lay out an array of additional real-life case studies of men I've encountered in my therapy practice. I'm interested in interrupting the assumption that sexual issues can be reduced to a single identifiable problem and easily solved. I acknowledge that as a sex therapist I encounter men who have identified sex as a problem — this is what's known as "the pathological bias," which recommends caution about generalizing about gay male sexuality based on my client population. At the same time, I'm interested in questioning and understanding the norms that exist in gay male sexual culture, how they have evolved over time, and how they interact not only with individual character styles but also with other cultural forces (race, media, technology, geography, age, education, ethnicity, disability, gender expression, and verbal ability, not to mention exposure to pornography). I see these questions and foibles and obstacles and conflicts around sex not as evidence of being defective but as evidence of being human.

There are case studies that can describe a course of treatment that results in success, as measured by substantial relief or the resolution of a dilemma. But I'm less invested in telling success stories than in acknowledging complications and expanding our ability to tolerate the vulnerabilities and the mysteries of sexual longing. As the playwright Wallace Shawn once said to me in an interview, "Sex is a way in which the mysterious forces of the universe find themselves inside predictable bourgeois lives and overthrow their predictability. It's a very powerful force that perhaps everyone else understands and I don't. Or perhaps nobody understands."

* * *

Paolo has been in a relationship for three years. He and his partner are having trouble connecting intimately, both physically and emotionally. Paolo works incessantly and doesn't reserve much time for personal connection. He told me on the phone that he wants to explore being more free with his partner sexually and he also wants to connect with his own energy more. He's a tall, handsome, well-spoken guy. The center of his concern is rapid ejaculation. He gets aroused fast and cums fast and so there's a lot of stress and not much pleasure around arousal. Once he feels the tiniest bit turned on, he goes into full-stress mode worrying about shooting. I gave him a thorough, slow, sensual massage. He let me know that when I touched around his butt, he started getting aroused. When I turned him over, I talked him through a bunch of different methods for moving energy around: shaking hands and feet, patting/smacking his body, making sounds, and alternating between taking slow and deep breaths, short and shallow breaths, and holding his breath. He dutifully practiced all these things and, bless his heart, he was able to stay aroused for almost half an hour without squirting. But when I checked it to see how it was for him, he said it was very stressful – apparently he was mentating nonstop about whether he was going to succeed at this or fail. So it was hard for this to register as pleasurable. But one step at a time. He said his partner just loves to fuck, and so they're very far apart sexually. The partner seems to have no patience for Paolo's situation. This is another instance of expecting your partner or yourself to Perform Like a Porn Star. I suggested they conduct some limited-time experiments as a way to ease toward each other — set a timer and spend 15 minutes giving each other back massages or foot rubs, or make out with their underwear on, or take turns watching each other self-pleasure — either as a prelude to lovemaking or as activities complete in themselves free of pressure to make something specific happen.

* * *

My client Tom had a beer with a friend named Mike who wants Tom to top him. Mike told him, "You're not very assertive," which brought Tom into contact (paradoxically) with his own sense of agency. In the past, words like assertiveness, potency, and masculinity were very fraught for him, but not so much right now. Mike shared a fantasy scenario of wanting Tom to tie him up and fuck him, and in the bar he said, "I feel like grabbing your crotch right now." Tom said, "Go ahead," and Mike refrained. As they further processed it, Mike admitted he wanted Tom to direct him with a certain command, which Tom described as "a boring Bound Gods soundtrack: 'Grab my crotch, boy!'." (Verb that noun!) Tom gave him some great instruction. "First of all, you don't tell a top how to top, and second of all, I did give you a command and you didn't respond to it." Mike realized he missed his chance, by being rigid and not present to the experience, so fixated was he on his porn script. Mike is far from alone — there are plenty of guys who are so accustomed to interacting with devices that they don't know how to talk directly to someone in person in a way that is organic, spontaneous, authentic, and unscripted.

* * *

Ross is very frustrated with the hookup culture that social media facilitate. Guys make dates and don't show up. They don't know how to have sex — they lie there like logs and expect him to do all the work. They want Ross's cock up their asses bare. He told me about having dinner with a smart, nice Irishman, and it seemed they were in agreement about not having sex on the first date. But he invited Ross up to his apartment on a ridiculous pretense – his pipes were frozen, he wanted to make sure they were okay. He went in the other room and came back completely naked.

* * *

Jeff said he's game for being verbal and negotiating with partners, but he's had a couple of bad experiences of speaking up and then the other guy disappearing forever, so he's a little skittish about that. To some extent, that's the oldest story in the book: guys are uncomfortable talking about sex. They just want to have the grunting and the fucking and then be done. But to the extent that sexual encounters these days reflect what's modeled in porn, that almost never includes conversation about what you feel or what you want.

* * *

Barry's tales from the dating wars are appalling. He told me about meeting a 25-year-old named P. on Adam4Adam who was home from college for a week and wanted Barry, a 52-year-old swimming instructor, to teach him to swim. Barry gave him three free lessons, loaned him a cap and goggles, and organized free entrance to two different gyms. P. made noises about wanting to take Barry to lunch and/or meet him at his apartment, theoretically for rolling around naked. He made two dates and cancelled both at short notice. Then he left town.

While Barry was waiting for the second date to happen, he got a message from someone he's been chatting with on A4A for over a year. The guy wanted to meet, and when Barry replied that he was supposed to get together with a friend and was waiting to hear if it would happen, the guy went ballistic on him: "gay guys are all alike, you asshole, etc." Barry wrote him back and said, "Your anger has nothing to do with me," and blocked him.

Vacationing in London, he was approached on Grindr by a guy who wanted to meet at Starbucks. Barry said no, let's meet at my hotel. He waited half an hour. When the guy didn't show up, Barry messaged him, and the guy wrote back saying something unavoidable came up. Barry wrote back to say, "You could have let me know rather than make me wait – that's bad manners." The guy wrote back saying, "What makes you think I'd meet you, Grandpa?"

Bad manners are timeless, and certainly online culture has grown its own varieties of rude comments and anonymous insults. But especially for younger guys, watching porn and cruising online have taught men to treat each other as if they were video-game avatars, not quite real people, objects without feelings. Barry and I talked about the fast-food intimacy aspect of hookup culture. The norm has become getting together without much conversation beforehand, which raises wild expectations based on wishful thinking but results in unsatisfying or aborted encounters.

* * *

James is an attractive 34-year-old professional. He's on his third relationship in two years where the sex has gone dead after about a month, and he knows it's his issue. "After a couple of months, I get turned off sexually. It's easier to have sex with strangers." Although his first relationship stayed sexual for 2½ years, his most recent relationship with Miguel broke up after four months because sex got scarce, although they've continued to date and have sex. He enjoys bottoming, giving and receiving oral sex. He knows that he fetishizes big dicks because his first boyfriend had a "perfect" dick. "I want a big dick to dominate me. I look at big dicks in porn every day." He jerks off once or twice every day and can get off in four minutes looking at XTube, where he searches for the keywords "huge cock." He tried going without porn for a week and noticed that he was hungrier for sex with Miguel.

    I reflected to James the pile-up of interlocking issues. One, he has an addictive personality. Two, he's subject to "spectatoring" during sex (dissociating from physical pleasure and viewing the encounter from outside his body). Three, the first boyfriend with the "perfect dick" created a strong imprint to which other partners are unconsciously compared, creating dangerously high expectations. And four, his deeply ingrained habit of looking at porn creates a rigid picture of what sex is and instills tremendous anxiety when he can't manage to reproduce his porn fantasy. Each of these issues can be addressed and carefully worked through, but there's no quick fix.

PORN AS SEX EDUCATION

Paradox: Porn is liberating because it shows the vast variety of possible sexual activities. It inspires creativity and imagination.

Porn is intimidating because it creates pressure to master every possible sexual activity.

My client Terry dated a guy named Devin for a short time. Their sexual chemistry was terrific, but Terry broke off the relationship because he couldn't handle Devin's periodic manifestation of effeminate mannerisms (what the playwright Paul Rudnick calls "nelly attacks"). Although Devin functioned masterfully as a top in bed, Terry dismissively referred to him as a "blouse." Lately, though, he's been missing the fun, the passion, and the intimacy they shared. It's hard for Terry to integrate or make equal space for that feeling of connection *and* his devotion to a certain masculine energy that is important for his sexual arousal. He acknowledges that he's addicted to the Craigslist/porn scenario of the dominant macho guy, making you do what he says, rewarding you by cumming in your mouth. His dilemma speaks to the question of whether gay male porn reflects our tastes or creates them. Terry's sexual behavior and his choice of partners may well stem from his genuine attraction to conventional, even stereotypical masculinity — a perfect example of what Jack Morin calls "your core erotic theme." But his brain has also been inundated with pictures and videos of sexual interaction between men who occupy a narrow stripe of male body types. We don't see too many porn clips featuring notably effeminate men masterfully fucking other men, even though it clearly happens in real life. The gap between what we see and what we feel perpetuates both the prizing of a certain idealized masculinity and the devaluing of bodies that don't live up to that ideal, which — let's face it — includes most of us.

* * *

If you came of age in the early to mid-1980s, gay = "Got AIDS Yet?" The mainstream media — national newsweekly magazines and network news — instilled young gay men with huge fears that even the slightest sexual contact led directly to a swift, painful, and ignominious death. At the same time, home video, cable TV, VCRs, and a proliferating gay media formed an alternative source of information. Looking at porn videos or reading erotic stories in slick magazines taught the basics of male-on-male sexual interaction, feeding the hunger for primary education. Viewed in the privacy of your own home, porn permitted and encouraged the flowering of sexual arousal and imagination without the danger of direct contact with another person, so no exposure to disease. Jerking off to porn was the ultimate safe sex and, who knows, may have spared a generation of men from the plague. The underground library of porn put on display a pleasurable variety of sexual options, more than you might encounter as a young man making your way through the gay sexual subculture. Watching it in private protected your public identity — you could explore gay life vicariously and discreetly without endangering whatever persona your social environment required you to adopt. You could engage with handsome, sexually dexterous porn stars for your own pleasure without the slightest fear that they would reject you. And with no audience to scrutinize your functioning or your techniques, you could enjoy sexual pleasure without any performance anxiety. There was nobody to get it up for, nobody to shoot for, nothing to prove.

* * *

Gay male porn allows straight people to find out about, accept, and enjoy gay sex. Some women (including lesbians) get off on watching gay male porn not only because it's hot but also because it's one of the few forms of porn that doesn't objectify/degrade women. It also shows men expressing desire and being physically affectionate toward one another (as opposed to insulting each other on Grindr), which women rarely get to see and can't get enough of. "Straight" or bi-curious men can check out gay male porn safely without having to identify publicly or risk stigma. When my client Enrique says, "What I like watching is porn about seducing a straight guy," I understand that for him gay male porn normalizes the experience of sexual fluidity, in contrast to many cultural and social contexts which rigidly enforce gender-role stereotypes and punish non-conformists. That's what makes gay male porn simultaneously comical, provocative, and subversive.

* * *

Another paradox is that viewing porn can both induce shame and pave the way to healing. Social researcher Brené Brown sat down with a therapist who had spent more than 25 years working with men. The therapist explained that from the time boys are eight to ten years old, they learn that initiating sex is their responsibility and that sexual rejection soon becomes the hallmark of masculine shame. He said, "Even in my own life, when my wife isn't interested, I still have to battle feelings of shame. It doesn't matter if I intellectually understand why she's not in the mood. I'm vulnerable and it's very difficult." When Brown asked him about his work around addiction and pornography, he gave her an answer that helped her understand that issue in an entirely new light. He said, "For five bucks and five minutes, you think you're getting what you need, and you don't have to risk rejection."

And yet looking at porn can also help to dispel shame. In his novel *The Golden Age of Promiscuity*, Brad Gooch writes, "A sci-fi feeling of being on another planet, an entirely gay planet, drew Sean back in a puff of memory to the 55th Street Playhouse, where he had seen a Jack Wrangler movie a week before. He forgot the title. In the movie, Wrangler, in tight jeans the shade of a powdery Alabama sky, was driving home through San Francisco. When Wrangler tuned in to his car radio, a station was broadcasting a gay announcer delivering only gay news. When he arrived home, the telephone repairman, the super, and the electrician were all different gay stereotypes. Predictably, Wrangler wound up in a sexual knot with each one. The movie impressed Sean mostly by its evocation of a science-fiction world in which everyone was gay."

* * *

Sheldon first contacted me saying he wanted to work on his issues around sex shame and body image.

I suspected it was a little-dick issue, which it was indeed, but from his email I was unprepared for how perky, charming, attractive, and friendly he turned out to be in person. He's 39, lives in Astoria with a roommate, and works as a consultant in the garment industry. He said that his fixation on his small dick and his body imperfection influences his worldview. I took a detailed sexual history and learned that he's had a string of boyfriends (he named at least six) with whom he had successful and pleasurable sexual relationships, with plenty of acceptance from them. Nevertheless, he has a hard time cuddling or sharing a bed with a lover overnight. He gets very mental, highly anxious, and sweats profusely. He looks at a lot of porn and jerks off one to three times a day. I couldn't help thinking that may be the main source of his anxiety: he expects himself to look and perform like a porn star because those are the images in his head. It's another variation on Terry's dilemma — Sheldon hasn't watched hours and hours of perky, charming guys with medium-sized or small dicks expressing concern about their dick size, receiving reassurance and affirmation from their partners, and then having fun and satisfying sex.

It is a peculiar consequence of our digital era that the vast store of information available online at our fingertips has come to represent some unassailable authority, to the point of superseding or cancelling out the truth of what we can see right in front of us. Not unlike drivers who have gotten so dependent on being given verbal instructions by their GPS devices that they can't compute what their eyeballs are telling them about the road conditions up ahead, guys who watch a lot of porn online mistake the umpty-zillion iterations of writhing bodies with the User's Manual for Doing Sex Right. They consciously or unconsciously endeavor to duplicate in bed the action that looks so hot onscreen. As French philosopher Jean Baudrillard put it, "The map precedes the territory." The two-dimensional map becomes more important than the three-dimensional reality. Porn can be great for generating arousal and displaying the rudiments of a sexual encounter. But it's like the flimsy page of drawings that's supposed to help you put together IKEA furniture – there are some crucial instructions missing. If you're unaccustomed to having someone in the room with your arousal, porn doesn't teach you how to send or receive signals of pleasure or displeasure, nor does it guide you through the various ways to adjust accordingly. One of the saddest sentences I've ever heard was from a 24-year-old client who said, "I watched twenty gangbangs online before I ever kissed a boy."

You can usually tell if a guy you're having sex with has a strong porn habit because neither his body nor his voice registers much response. This is the biggest complaint I hear from guys about their casual sex partners: "He just lies there like a lump and expects me to do all the work." Or if he does make sound, he imitates the not-especially-articulate verbalizing from porn, which ranges from "Fuck!" to "Oh, fuck!" As de facto sex education, porn also teaches guys unconsciously to equate getting naked with having sex and to equate having sex with getting off, and let nothing stop that relentless trajectory!

* * *

I want to be careful to avoid making a mistake that's endemic to cultural criticism. When surveying the impact of pornography (or television or the internet) on contemporary culture, it's easy to fall into using language that conflates users' experience with some notion of intentionality on the part of technology.

"Television makes people stop reading books," for example, or "The internet has given us all attention deficit disorder." Pornography doesn't have the power to do things on its own. It is a consumer product that people view for their own purposes. If I speak of porn doing this or teaching that, consider that shorthand for "viewing porn" or "using porn."

That porn is a consumer product has everything to do with what porn does and doesn't show. One of the main reasons we don't see, for instance, the post-climax cuddling and cleaning up in porn movies is that it costs money to shoot those scenes and adds zero value to the movie from a consumer standpoint. If people really wanted to see those parts – if, say, a free amateur site like XTube showed a huge spike in people producing and watching the post-cum cuddle and cleanup scenes – then porn studios would start churning out the stuff for paying customers. (You loved watching some random guy in Pittsburgh towel the load off his stomach, but you'd pay to watch your favorite porn star do it!) Consumer demand has likely been a factor in pushing porn in the other direction, to showing less and less of the "full scene" and more and more of the specific moments people get off to: compilations of nothing but 500 facials in 50 minutes, 100 cumshots in 100 minutes, nothing but piss/fisting/flogging/deep throat/double penetration, etc. The rise of streaming porn (as opposed to DVD/VHS/film) means that people want more and more two-minute clips, rather than 20-minute scenes or 80-minute movies. The fact that this is a commercial product helps explain a lot of what porn includes and excludes.

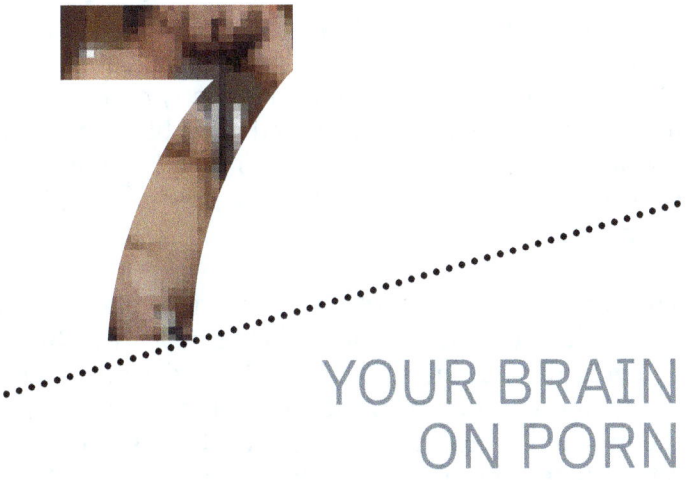

YOUR BRAIN ON PORN

Heterosexual commentary rarely foregrounds the liberating aspects of pornography, but some of its critique applies as much to gay male experience as it does to heterosexual men's. In her book-length diatribe *Pornland: How Porn Has Hijacked our Sexuality*, feminist academic Gail Dines writes, "Our pop culture resembles the soft-core pornography of ten years ago....As pop culture begins to look more and more pornographic, the actual porn industry has had to become more hard-core as a way to distinguish its products from those images found on MTV, in *Cosmopolitan*, and on billboards.

"What troubles many men most," Dines continues, "is that they need to pull up the porn images in their head in order to have an orgasm with their partner. They replay porn scenes in their mind or think about having sex with their favorite porn star when they are with their partners." She talks about a guy who was concerned about his sexual performance with women:

" 'I can't get the pictures of anal sex out of my head when having sex, and I am not really focusing on the girl but on the last anal scene I watched.' I asked him if he thought porn had in any way affected his sexuality, to which he answered, 'I don't know. I started looking at porn before I had sex, so porn is pretty much how I learned about sex. It can be a kind of problem to think about porn as much as I do, especially when with my girlfriend. It means I am not really present with her, my head is somewhere else.' "

* * *

This dilemma is beautifully dramatized in Joseph Gordon-Levitt's brave, honest film *Don Jon* (2013) in which he plays a smart, sexy guy addicted to porn. "I'm not gonna lie," he says in the monologue that opens the movie, the voiceover we hear while he engages in his favorite pastime with the help of his laptop. "This gets me hard as a fucking rock."

> *But I don't like to go too fast right off the bat. I'd rather work my way into it, nice and easy. So I'll start off with some stills. Then, once I'm getting into it, I start looking for a video. I never actually touch my cock til I find the right clip. Then once I do – goodbye. The next few minutes, all the bullshit fades away, and the only thing in the world is those tits…that ass…the blowjob, the cowboy, the doggy, the money shot, and that's it. I don't gotta say anything, I don't do anything I just fucking lose myself.*
>
> *There's only a few things I really care about in life. My body, my pad, my ride, my family, my church, my boys, my girls, and my porn. I know that last one sounds weird, but I'm just being honest. Nothing else does it for me the same way.*

Not even real pussy. And yo I get plenty of that. Why you think my boys call me the Don?

See, this is what I'm saying. Real pussy's all good. But I'm sorry. It's not as good as porn. Tits? Great. Ass? Great. Blowjob? Sure, it's fucking fantastic in person...if she'll do it. But in real life, if you wanna get head, you gotta give head. I know, some guys love eating pussy, but the thing about those guys is, they're fucking crazy. Don't get me wrong, I like a good pussy-eating clip. But from down here, there's nothing good about this. And if she does finally decide to do you the big favor, she's in a fucking hurry. Now when it come to the actual fucking, first of all, condoms are terrible, they just are. But you gotta wear one, cause unlike porn, real pussy can kill you. Second of all, missionary is the worst position in all of fucking. The tits lie flat, you can't see her ass, you can't touch her ass, 'cause she's lying on her back. They won't let you do it from behind 'cause they wanna look at you. And *basically it's on me to do all the work. Money shot? No. there is no real-life moneyshot. Real girls won't do that shit. You just gotta cum into the fucking condom. So you tell me, which looks better?*

* * *

In his 2012 TED Talk "The Great Porn Experiment," physiology professor Gary Wilson addresses the impact of watching online porn on the brains and sexual functioning of young heterosexual men. His analysis impresses me as sufficiently thorough and pertinent that I'm going to spend some time summarizing his findings. "Canadian researcher Simon Lajeunesse found that most boys seek pornography by age 10, driven by a brain that is suddenly fascinated by sex," says Wilson, the author of *Your Brain on Porn: Internet Pornography and the Emerging Science of Addiction*. "Now, users perceive internet porn as far more compelling than porn of the past. Why is that? Unending novelty. With internet porn, a guy can see more hot babes in 10 minutes than his ancestors could see in several lifetimes. The problem is he has a hunter-gatherer brain. A heavy-user brain rewires itself to this genetic bonanza so it carefully becomes associated with this porn harem. Such behaviors that are associated with this are being alone, voyeurism, clicking, searching, multiple tabs, fast-forwarding, constant novelty, shock, and surprise." These habits develop in contrast to and sometimes to the exclusion of the behaviors involved in real sex, such as "courtship, touching, being touched, smells, pheromones, emotional connection, interaction with a real person."

How does watching porn become addictive? Wilson talks about the "reward circuit" in the human brain that evolved to drive us towards natural rewards such as sex, bonding, and food. "Extreme versions of natural rewards have a unique ability to capture us. For example: high-calorie foods or hot novel babes give us extra dopamine. Too much dopamine, though, can override our natural satiation mechanisms." He goes on to cite experiments with giving rats unlimited access to junk food. "Almost all of them will binge to obesity," he says. "This is also why 4 out of 5 Americans are overweight and about half of those are obese. That is, addicted to food. In contrast to the natural rewards, drugs such as cocaine or alcohol only hook about 10% of users whether they are rats or humans. This binge mechanism for food or sex was once an evolutionary advantage. But what if mating season never ends? All those hits of dopamine can tell your brain to kick in a molecular switch called Delta-FosB, which starts to accumulate in the brain's reward circuit. Now, with excess chronic consumption of drugs or natural rewards, this buildup of Delta-FosB starts to alter the brain and promote the cycle of binging and craving. If the binging continues, the Delta-FosB builds up and it can lead to brain changes seen in all addicts. So the dominoes are: excess consumption, excess dopamine, Delta-FosB, brain changes.

"One of the first changes is a numbed pleasure response," Wilson says. "It kicks in so everyday pleasures really don't satisfy a porn addict. At the same time, other physical changes in the brain make the brain hyper-reactive to porn. Everything else in a porn user's life is sort of boring, but porn is super-exciting. Finally, his willpower erodes as his frontal cortex changes."

It's possible to reverse these changes in the brain, says Wilson, but only by giving up looking at porn. "Probably you want to know why any porn-loving guy in his right mind would give it up. Two words: erectile dysfunction. Internet porn is killing young men's sexual performance. Young guys are flaming out with women. Sexual enhancement drugs often stop working for these guys, if they ever did, because the problem isn't below the belt where Viagra works. Nor is their problem really psychological. It's due to physical changes in the brain. Their numb brains are sending weaker and weaker signals to their bananas."

Wilson refers to Italian urologist Dr. Carlo Foresta, whose research in recent years has centered on the negative impact of online porn on the sexual functioning of young men between the ages of 19 and 25. Foresta marks the decline in three progressive stages that starts with lower reactions to porn sites and proceeds to a general drop in libido. Ultimately, it becomes impossible to get an erection. "There are three takeaways from this," says Wilson. "First, Foresta is describing a classic addiction process — gradual desensitization. Second, internet porn is qualitatively different from *Playboy*. Widespread youthful ED has never been seen before. And finally ED is often the only symptom that gets these guys' attention. The question is what lesser symptoms are they missing? Most don't figure that out until after they quit."

In response to the physical changes caused by obsessive-compulsive porn consumption, some young men have taken it upon themselves to launch a movement called NoFap to encourage and support each other in breaking an unhealthy, addictive attachment to masturbating to porn. ("Fapping" is millennial slang for "jerking off.") The trademarked website NoFap.com hosts short- and long-term challenges in which participants abstain from porn and masturbation (for a week, a month, a year, a lifetime) with the clearly stated intentions to "recover from porn-induced sexual dysfunction, stop objectifying and establish meaningful connections, improve your interpersonal relationships, and live a more fulfilling life."

The website encourages visitors to maintain online journals chronicling their experiences attempting to abstain from PMO (Masturbating to Orgasm using Pornography) in order to reverse their PIED (Porn-Induced Erectile Dysfunction). The journals reflect how intricately looking at pornography is bound up with the use of substances (especially marijuana and alcohol) to soothe depression, social anxiety, and work and academic stress. Contributors meticulously monitor their habits, their temptations, the state of their erections, their wet dreams, their fluctuating between numbness and sensation, and their periods of low libido ("flatlining"). Here's a typical entry from a gay guy in his twenties:

> *If I am not attentive, my attempts to quit become an intense game of whack-a-mole. I stop watching porn for extended periods, but smoke more weed and surf grindr. I'll find myself surfing craigslist and posting, just for the thrill of receiving pictures. These are substitutions and prevent me making quality connections, but are disguised as ways to make connections. I quit porn July 7th, but continued substituting grindr and CL until just last week. This was largely due to a terrible flatline (yes, even using grindr and CL, I flatlined without porn). I felt like garbage, but also knew that I needed to push through. Recently, however, I have been having incredible dreams and often waking up with a morning chub...As I start to feel better, I become more tempted to return to casual habits, but I intend to use my time to complete more work and renew quality connections.*

Based on his research from an addiction perspective, Gary Wilson notes that guys in their early twenties aren't regaining their erectile health as quickly as older guys. Even though older guys have been using porn longer, they didn't start on today's internet porn. Research indicates that older guys didn't start having sexual problems until after they got high-speed internet. "Today's young teens start on high-speed internet when their brains are at their peak of dopamine production and neuroplasticity. This is also when they are the most vulnerable to addiction, but there is another risk. By adulthood, teens strengthen heavily-used circuits and prune back unused ones. So, by age 22 or so a guy's sexual taste can be like deep roots in his brain. This can cause panic if a guy has escalated to extreme porn or porn that no longer matches his sexual orientation. Fortunately, brains are plastic so his taste can revert once he quits porn. As a guy returns to normal sensitivity his brain looks around for the rewards it evolves to see, such as friendly interaction and of course real mates."

Other commentators have questioned the scientific validity of studying sexual behavior the same way as drug and alcohol addictions. In an article republished online by *Psychology Today*, clinical psychologist David J. Ley makes the case that the high levels of brain activity that anti-porn advocates pathologize as addiction could also signal healthy adults with high libidos. I side with those who prefer not to apply the terminology of addiction to sexual behavior, partly for semantic reasons. Alcohol and drug dependencies are defined by their ability to be quantitatively measured and treated in a way that sexual behavior cannot, even if compulsive cruising and out-of-control porn-watching leads to similarly negative consequences on social behavior and sexual functioning. I'm also aware that what constitutes normal/acceptable/healthy sexual behavior relies heavily on the values of the observer. Wilson's talk and the studies he cites deal exclusively with heterosexual men and so have nothing to say about the ways that pornography has historically played an important role in validating the desires and experience of non-heterosexual men.

In contrast to Wilson's research, the refreshingly colloquial British gay publication *FS* (published by the health charity Gay Men Fighting AIDS) conducted an admittedly unscientific study of gay men's porn habits. More than 1000 readers responded, 87% of whom watched porn at least once a week. One in four watched porn every day. Although the report acknowledged that some men felt out of control with their porn-viewing, the study reflected more concern about the impact of bareback porn on gay men's sexual behavior offline than with issues of addiction. One in 14 men in the magazine's survey indicated that watching bareback porn increased their willingness to engage in unprotected anal sex. And the contrast between the stimulating sight of bareback fucking and the less-stimulating sensation of latex-protected sex was cited as a potential factor in impaired sexual functioning. "I only watch bareback porn, and I realized recently that I've been finding it difficult to maintain an erection while having sex," noted a study participant named James. "I always seem to lose it as I put the condom on. So now I'm thinking, is it down to the amount of bareback porn I watch? I've nearly put myself at risk several times, too, because I couldn't keep it hard."

It's not just men whose sexual pleasure gets compromised by long-term exposure to pornography. Although here I am primarily concerned with talking about gay men's sex lives, I was intrigued to read sexologist Paul Joannides's comments in the online journal *Contemporary Sexuality* about the impact of pornography on young women. "We live in a world where most people believe it's normal for young women to have sex. So why do a number of women today think that masturbation is nasty? I blame it on the unfortunate state of sex education, which for many young adults is little more than a bizarre combination of abstinence-only curricula and porn," wrote Joannides, author of the doorstop-sized manual *The Guide to Getting It On!* "For women, this has resulted in a heavy dose of shame from the abstinence-only side of things, mixed with the idea taken from porn that the only good girl is a girl gone wild. In porn, good sex happens magically whenever a guy pulls out a penis. Nowhere is there a healthy middle ground. We don't help young women understand how to become more comfortable with their sexual selves. No one is encouraging young women to explore their bodies on their own. No one is giving them permission to learn about their own sexual responsiveness without a partner present."

It's undeniable that there are plenty of people whose social and sexual functioning has been damaged by excessive porn-watching. Taking a break is sometimes essential, if easier said than done.

HITTING THE PAUSE BUTTON

I first met Brian on Scruff. We fooled around a couple of times, and he hired me for a couple of erotic massages. Then one day he contacted me because he was in a pleasure crisis. He's 34, and after four years of looking at porn daily for professional reasons (one of his freelance writing gigs was blogging for a porn site), he gave up porn two weeks ago. Since then, he's not able to masturbate "to completion." At first it was difficult even to get hard. He's been accustomed to ending the day jerking off; now he finds he's more tired than horny at bedtime. He can get off having sex, which gives him an advantage over guys who can't get off with partners because of their deeply ingrained habits of jerking off to porn.

Brian has always loved his self-pleasuring. It's a treasured aspect of his erotic existence. As he put it, in his characteristically colorful way, "I slapped my salami as often as possible, but I've only done it in the company of visual stimulation for as long as I can remember. In high school I had underwear catalogs and Cinemax after midnight. Then, after getting a job in a bookstore, I purloined stroke mags that were supposed to be mailed back to the distributor. In college I graduated to VHS tapes before DVDs took over. Then, when the internet hit, I had every type of porn known to man just sitting there in my room, waiting for me to masturbate to it." In recent years he's developed an elaborate routine of spending 20 minutes or so at the end of the day looking at porn and jerking off, maybe four times a week, usually solo, sometimes with a buddy. In bed with his laptop, with Elbow Grease and towel nearby, he likes to look at fucking (especially bareback), rough sex, verbal scenes, and anything involving muscular guys like ginger pornstar James Jamesson.

After four years of blogging about porn, he noticed that his pleasure had turned into boredom, which signaled time to give it a break. I coached him through a variety of body-awareness practices aimed at rebooting his erotic organism: self-massage, breathing, making sound, combining cock-stroking with touching the rest of his body. His awareness of the benefits was slight at first because he was so acclimated to the high-powered hot-wiring of porn, but he was motivated to undertake a different kind of erotic workout and within a couple of weeks was able to report a return to pleasurable masturbation. He blogged about his experience so entertainingly that I'm going to let him speak about it in his own words:

> *I called my friend Don Shewey, a writer and sex therapist, who I figured might be able to cure me of my porn addiction. After talking to him about my past habits and current predicament, he told me that my mind was so used to the excess stimulation*

of bodies rutting on screen that it was having trouble remembering how to enjoy a good old fashioned stroke like my grandparents used to. He suggested breaking all of my usual habits. He told me to experiment with a new time of day, new positions, new lube and maybe even some new hand movements to shock myself out of complacency. We did some "body awareness" exercises, where I explored parts of myself other than the organs surrounding the taint to see what else gave me an erotic charge. He also taught me some new strokes – taking your dick and rubbing it with both hands like you're trying to start a fire sounds ridiculous until you give it a whirl.

All of those things helped, but the most important thing he told me was to not worry about squirting. I should enjoy playing with myself just for how good it made me feel, he said. With that advice, I started self-molestation all the time... I wasn't getting off, but the exploration was fun. It was like when you're an adolescent and have that uncontrollable desire to put your hand down your pants, coupled with the idea that what you're doing is the filthiest thing on Earth. There's no bigger turn-on than breaking the rules.

After about a week of not shooting a wad (stupid boyfriend and his damn business trips!) I was horny as fuck and distracting myself by innocently cleaning out the drawers in my dresser. That's when I found them in the bottom of the junk drawer: three old porn mags. I don't know why I saved these mid-90s dinosaurs, but after six weeks of seeing only my boyfriend's cock and the occasional glimpse in the locker room, I couldn't help taking a stroll down memory lane.

It was like the first time I saw porn all over again. A rod stronger than He-Man and firmer than the hair on Jersey Shore popped in my pants almost immediately. I was excited and aroused and, *because of the ban, felt like I was breaking some sort of rule (again, always the biggest turn on). Then, while rubbing my jeans and scanning the pages, I was consumed by an overwhelming sense of guilt about breaking my self-imposed smut celibacy.*

I threw the mags away, but I couldn't get rid of my boner so easily. I decided to try everything that Don had told me: a new room in the house (bathroom), a new position (sitting perilously on the edge of the tub), some different lube (something called Stroke 29)… As I had done for the past few weeks, I enjoyed it for just what it was, but after a couple of minutes I knew I was finally going to cross the finish line (and after a week, what a finish line that was).

While cleaning up I felt triumphant, albeit in a sort of Lance Armstrong-y way. Yes, porn had given me the initial, um, courage, but I relied on all my other senses and training to get the job done. Maybe this was a way of weaning myself off? I decided this meant I wasn't 100 percent cured, but I was definitely on the way to becoming porn-free.

I finally reached my goal at the eight-week mark. While sitting around the house, I figured I'd go touch myself just for kicks like I had been doing for weeks. As soon as I tapped my rod I could tell this time was different. My left hand, which is usually as useless as a pork shoulder in a kosher kitchen, started to get in on the action, pleasuring parts of my body that had never gone inside another human. Nipple tweaking, thigh-grabbing, ball-stretching – I was like a one-man visit to a back room. I closed my eyes and didn't think about porn or sex or anything – just felt all the things my skin could feel, focusing on what my body was telling me and how good it felt.

Yes, it sounds more annoying and new age-y than an Enya song stuck on loop, but it's true. It was like getting back to basics. I realized this wasn't going to be one of my fruitless romps with myself, and as I felt the conclusion welling up, I pulled away, happy to let the fun go on for as long as possible. Jerking off suddenly wasn't a chore – it had nothing to do with work – it was like an all-you-can-eat buffet of fun. After a while I became a little bit afraid I would lose it for good, so I pulled the trigger on one of the better orgasms I've ever had. I didn't weigh myself afterward, but I probably lost about half a pound.

A few days later, when the need for some self-flagellation arose, I decided to give porn another shot. It was quick, easy and, as always, fun. I had proved I didn't need it, I just wanted it. Yeah, I might have found enlightenment by giving up porn for a couple of months, but I wasn't going to scrap it altogether. I may be crazy, but I'm not stupid.

I am always impressed, inspired, and moved by anyone who chooses to sacrifice short-term pleasures for long-term mental and physical well-being, especially when they have as much fun as Brian had conducting the experiment. It takes tremendous courage and self-compassion — not to mention support from others — to stop drinking, to stop doing drugs, or to make a profound change in sexual behavior, including looking at pornography. I want to be a resource and a champion for anyone for whom that's a good choice to make.

9
PORN AS IMAGINATION EDUCATION

Pornography does a lousy job if you try to use it as a sex manual. It excels, however, when it comes to educating the erotic imagination. To adolescents, pornography speaks darker and deeper truths about bodies the way fairy tales thrill young readers by acknowledging that life is full of scary things — the information that schoolbooks and parents try to protect kids from but that shows up anyway in their fearful fantasies and bad dreams.

"Super-hero comic books were the porn of my childhood," queer sex advice columnist Pat Califia wrote in an essay published in *The Advocate*. "My first fist-fucking magazine was not as thrilling as those brightly-colored, fantastic adventures on sleazy newsprint. The images of capture, helplessness and torture were the most exciting: Superman being drained of his strength by Kryptonite, Aquaman dying slowly in a net hung over a swimming pool, Sheena tied upside down and being threatened with a hot spearpoint. In bed, I dreamed of flying through space, being gifted with strange powers which required me to do battle with evil, being imprisoned and tortured by enemies who were somehow near and familiar to me, then being magically and inevitably released.

"When I got older and my reading skills improved," Califia continued, "I discovered more explicit material in Zane Grey (a woman tied to a horse, her blouse ripped off, and the horse sent galloping into a forest fire), Pearl Buck (rough soldiers raping a graceful and beautiful boy — the Imperial Woman carried to her curtained bed by her childhood sweetheart), and Henry Miller (a woman reaching under a banquet table to fondle another woman's genitals). There were also historical accounts of Indian torture, the Spanish Inquisition and psychiatric textbooks. Upon discovering indecencies in these circumspect volumes, I would blush and wonder if I were the only person to find anything titillating about them. If I was not, how on earth did they manage to stay on the shelves?

"I turned to the library because none of the adults I knew would talk to me about sex, beyond sketching the anatomy of reproduction. I needed to know much more than that: I needed to know about pleasure. I was tormented by lust, which had taken on a new and bittersweet urgency with adolescence. I had little idea what people did about these tempests of need, and I was very sure that the least move to still my frustration would have disastrous consequences. My gleanings of erotica and frequent, guilt-ridden masturbation were all that kept me sane until I escaped parental supervision."

As a writer raised in a strict Mormon household, Califia (a formerly lesbian author and BDSM champion who later came out as a transman and eventually a parent himself) has thought a lot about how family and culture affect the formation of young people's erotic imagination. "Since parents are confronted daily with their children's curiosity about sex and enthusiasm for vigorous physical activity and strong sensations, it is a wonder that they manage to be such hypocrites about it. A form of culturally induced schizophrenia allows them to make sentimental speeches about the fleeting innocence of childhood and the happiness of years unburdened by responsibility of carnal lust, then to turn around and spend an incredible amount of time policing the sex lives of their children. Children are celibate because their parents prevent them from playing with other little kids or adults. They are shy because they are not allowed to go naked any longer than is absolutely necessary to take a bath. They are not innocent, they are ignorant, and that ignorance is deliberately created and maintained by parents who won't answer questions about sex and often punish their children for being bold enough to ask. This does not make sex disappear. The erotic becomes a vast, unmapped wilderness whose boundaries are clearly delineated by averted eyes. Sex becomes the thing not seen, the word not spoken, the forbidden impulse, the action that must be denied."

Another lesbian author, Amber Hollibaugh, has written eloquently about a gay kid's need to find external sources to help make sense of sex and the body, imagination and identity. "When I was younger, I tried to control my imagination more strictly than my sex life; my mind scared me much more than the actual things I was doing in bed. No one had ever told me that I could explore fantasy without ever going farther than the dreamings. I really believed that if an image rested at the corners of my mind, giving it center stage would inevitably lead to doing it," she wrote. "It is a bitter irony to me that I was in my mid-thirties before anyone explained to me that I was not what I dreamed, that fantasies had a reality of their own and did not necessarily lead anywhere but back to themselves. I had never understood that I might be deeply fascinated by an idea in my mind and not enjoy it at all if I actually tried it, that fantasy could give me a way to picture different aspects of my own growing sexual consciousness (or exploit my lover's) without going any farther. Or that it would allow me a freedom that is unhindered by the limits of my body or the boundaries of my conscience. In my life I need monogamy but am free to experiment with an army of lovers in my mind. In reality I am limited to a certain number of orgasms done in a particular sequence, but in my mind I am capable of infinite climaxes and paths to satisfaction. I am often shocked by my own sexual world. It is much denser and more forbidden than I knew. But it is also richer and has helped me find the beginnings of the words that might make sex of the body as complex and satisfying as my dreams of it. It has begun to give me back sensation in my body that had been lost for years."

In the process of acquiring a worldly education through exposure to literature, visual art, pop culture, and other cultural artifacts, pornography serves a purpose by making space for sexual fantasies whether they get enacted or not. Like science fiction and fantasy literature and films, its power can be measured by how far it stretches the imagination beyond your personal experience or even what's physically possible or realistically desirable. According to a 1983 sex study, "coercion ranks with group sex and anonymity in the basic repertoire of sexual reverie," wrote Richard Goldstein in the *Village Voice*. "Dreams of romantic interludes, the meat and potatoes of pulp fiction for women, ranked far behind fantasies of rape and promiscuity...What folks want in a stroke book (or film) is freedom from the trammels of personality. Those who long for realism in pornography — ordinary acts with plausible partners — ought to be condemned to dream that way. What we want, in those moments of escape from tangibility, is excess and extremity."

There is a qualitative difference between written porn and artistic renderings of sexual activities (drawings, paintings, and sculptures) — which have an abstraction to them that requires filling in by the imagination — and pornographic photographs, films, and streaming video online, which are easier to identify with and harder to abstract. And there is clearly a generational divide between those who grew up with instant, ubiquitous access to porn online and those who didn't. Robert Christgau, who falls in the latter category, wrote in the *Village Voice*, "In my life, the analytic (not to mention contemplative) detachment of porn has not only been enjoyable in itself but has intensified my erotic-emotional involvement." Meanwhile, in a recent issue of *Psychotherapy Networker*, Ian Kerner reported that 99 percent of boys and 86 percent of girls have already seen porn by the time they reach the age of 16. "We're also seeing young male clients who are so used to the novelty and visual stimulation of Internet porn that it's harder for them to sustain prolonged lovemaking and stay connected to an actual flesh-and-blood partner. The term I've coined to describe all that is Sexual Attention Deficit Disorder (SADD). Men with SADD tend to find themselves getting bored or impatient during sex and suffering from mechanical 'male-functions': they may be *physiologically* aroused and even have an erection, but they're not at peak *mental* arousal. Guys with SADD may simply lack the mojo for real sex because they're depleted from masturbation. They're not running on a full tank, physically, mentally, and certainly not sexually."

Another paradox: porn can stimulate the fantasy-forming function of the brain, and it can also deaden fantasizing by inundating the brain with overly literal representations of sex.

Randall and Alejandro have been together seven years. They came to see me because they wanted help spicing up their sex life. What that really means is that they want it to resemble the porn they watch. And they have quite different tastes and styles of interacting with porn. Alejandro, who's 32, jerks off two or three times a week, spending 20-30 minutes at a time watching Daddy porn on oldmanboytube.com. Randall, who's 45, rarely jerks off but may spend 15-20 minutes a week looking at bareback porn on gaymaletube. Alejandro likes dirty talk and would like Randall to verbalize what he's feeling while they're having sex. Randall would like to develop a vocabulary to be more verbal during sex but it doesn't come naturally. Alejandro gave him some samples to study, featuring verbally dominant, swaggering tops saying things like, "You like my big cock? What? Louder! Say the alphabet while you're sucking me! That's right, P, as in Plow your ass, which is what I'm about to do," etc. Randall dutifully studied the video and gave it his best shot. But then Alejandro complained that he sounded mechanical, not engaged. I gently suggested that Alejandro wasn't being present with the actual Randall. He was expecting him to Perform Like a Porn Star, to duplicate the fantasy. He was using the porn as a test rather than an inspiration, which was a boner-kill for Randall.

This is a dilemma many couples face, and it isn't immediately obvious how to incorporate fantasy into sex. It is doable, according to Pat Califia, but it requires imagination more than imitation. "I found that sex is always a dry lesson in anatomy until it is infused with the erotic imagination," Califia wrote. "The inner voice of eros is arbitrary, bizarre, impeccably honest, bountiful and so powerful as to be cruel. It takes courage to hear its demands and follow them. Because I sensed a connection between private fantasy and good sex, I did not abandon my smutty 'home movies' as I learned how to persuade others to join me in sensual exploration... I continued to enrich, diversify and embroider my fantasies. Today, reading porn (or erotica, if you enjoy euphemisms) and plying my vibrator are as important to me as the sex I have with lovers, friends and tricks. I prefer partners who do not make hard and fast distinctions between masturbation and lovemaking, between what we can think of and what we can do, who are willing to risk their dignity in pursuit of delight."

10 PORN AND BODY STANDARDS

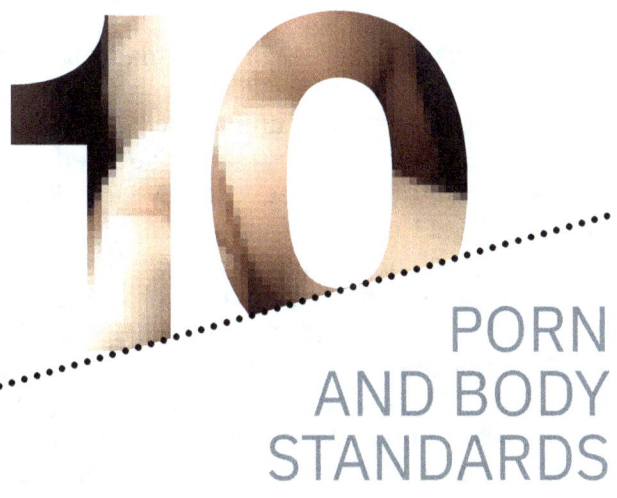

"When I was 21 or 22 in the late '70s, I remember walking past the Saint and seeing this line of clones waiting to get in, and I thought, 'These people don't look so bad. I'd like to sleep with most of them. Why am I hiding like this?' I've spent most of my life dealing with being overweight. I got very angry when I saw David Drake's piece [The Night Larry Kramer Kissed Me], *when he talks about going to the gym to turn himself into a warrior. There's a way in which I've always felt radically disaffected with the gay community, feeling on a very personal level not attractive and devalued as a result of that. I have a great deal of anger about it. I love Paul Monette's work, but I was reading a novel where this guy with AIDS falls in love with this man who's 50. I thought, 'Thank God, a novel that isn't about Joe Twinkie and John Twinkie who meet at the gym doing their 50th rep of whatever.' The guy takes his clothes off, and the guy with AIDS looks at him and says, 'There's not an ounce of fat on*

him.' And it's like, 'At 50? Please!' I thought at least when I was 50....! Why don't I just kill myself now?"
—*playwright Tony Kushner*

Porn is for gay men what fashion magazines are for women: a stylized commercial showcase for beauty that has the unfortunate, unintended effect of setting an impossibly high, unconsciously adopted standard for what constitutes physical attractiveness. Beginning in the 1920s, Hollywood imprinted the world with the concept of movie-star good looks, centered on gorgeous faces. The male pantheon includes such icons as Cary Grant and Clark Gable, Marlon Brando and Paul Newman. Each generation contributes a new face or two. Starting in the 1970s, the bodybuilding culture went mainstream along with the fitness craze, bringing a new emphasis on men's muscles and shapeliness, bulging pecs and washboard abs. But at least movie stars and bodybuilders kept their drawers on. Pornography exposed everything in the swimsuit region to heightened scrutiny and invidious comparison.

Of course, any woman in her right mind knows that fashion models — the Kate Mosses, Naomi Campbells, and Linda Evangelistas of the world — constitute a tiny fraction of the female population. And they can probably put it together that those flawless exteriors come at a high price, literally and figuratively: freakish genetics, who knows what kind of cosmetic surgery, starvation diets and/or eating disorders, groomers and makeup artists and clever lighting and retouch wizardry costing beaucoup de bucks. Nevertheless, when *every* magazine spread and *every* advertisement and *every* commercial and *every* billboard and *every* Hollywood movie and *every* TV news broadcast foregrounds the same sleek super-beauty, a norm gets established. It requires extraordinary strength and self-possession to question and reject or maintain some sense of perspective and independence from that mythical realm.

Likewise, intelligent gay men only have to look around to know that there are 150 different body types in the world. And yet extreme body-consciousness (aka body-snobbery aka body fascism) has long been a key feature in gay male culture. However it showed up before, whether in gym attendance or advertising, the ubiquity of pornography has amplified it exponentially. The handful of physical attributes that show up in gay male porn have become the gold standard against which everyone else measures themselves and comes up short. Naturally, it's fun to look at good-looking guys having sex. It's an act of public service for handsome men in good shape with great haircuts, strong muscular bodies, wide shoulders, narrow waists, beautiful beefy butts, and large high-functioning cocks to display themselves in public for all to witness and admire.

But when the same Ken-doll body shows up again and again, in porn videos and porn stills and advertisements for all products and in photo spreads taken at gay clubs and in headless profile pics on Grindr, there's a natural tendency to glorify that one type and judge all others as inferior. Reason flies out the window. There becomes a wider and wider gap between the men who will take off their shirts at the beach and the men who won't, the men who will let their dicks be seen in the locker room at the gym and those who won't. What is widely visible becomes the only look that is permissible; all else must hide. We make up these strange rules for ourselves: No pecs, no sex. Nobody could love me or desire me if I don't look like (Name Porn Star) or a Calvin Klein underwear ad photographed by Bruce Weber. Sex is for the young and beautiful. Or just the young.

The paradox of pornography is that we love looking at men who are unusually hot, handsome, well-built, muscled, shapely, hung, masculine, exhibitionistic, and sexually adventurous — we know they're extraordinary and we admire them for that. But when you spend a lot of time looking at gay porn images online, every day, maybe hours a day, for years, and don't spend very much time in the company of naked men in real life, those porn bodies start to become ordinary, the norm. They're all you know. It's possible to fall into this strange trance where you believe that every gay guy has an enormous dick and bulging biceps and sculpted abs and tattoos and piercings and pubic hair trimmed like topiary and the ability to take a fist and forearm up his ass... every gay guy except you, that is, in which case why would you even dare to leave the house, let alone hook up with someone or go on a date? You're only setting yourself up to disappoint your partner, who will surely reject you. And so we groom ourselves in the distorted mirror of porn.

* * *

Speaking of grooming: in addition to portraying a rather narrow range of bodies, porn also conveys some peculiar ideas about how body grooming and body hair can/should look. For example, nobody in porn has a hairy back. Most hairy chests, and pretty much all pubes and armpits and assholes, are clippered and trimmed. Even the guys who read as "hairy" in most porn don't actually have that much fur, and what they do have is neatly trimmed and groomed. So to the extent that guys who watch a lot of porn play monkey-see monkey-do, it's not just about achieving the perfect body but also committing to constant grooming. You are never done striving to achieve this body because even if you can get there it requires perpetual maintenance. A lot of guys study those bodies, consciously or unconsciously, and spend hours grooming themselves so they don't have that awful body hair that qualifies as secondary masculine characteristics. (Never mind ear hair, nose hair, bushy eyebrows, hairy knuckles...)

Beyond body types, there are also body colors. Porn communicates a very limited notion of how race and ethnicity works, playing to ethnic stereotypes about what kind of guys are hot for certain acts. Black guys are hot as tops, especially if they're fucking white guys. Asian guys almost never appear, but if they do, they're bottoms. Latin guys (note: never specifically "Mexican" or "Cuban" or "Peruvian," since those nationalities apparently carry no sexual charge here... maybe Puerto Rican or Brazilian, but otherwise generically "Latin") are also tops, particularly valued for their uncut cocks. Jewish guys are entirely invisible. Jewish performers tend to use Italian porn names, operating on the assumption that you may want a Jewish boyfriend, but everyone wants to get fucked by an Italian. Porn viewers—particularly non-white viewers—internalize all sort of messages about how they are meant to appear, what they are expected to do in bed, and what attributes they are valued/fetishized for as sex partners.

* * *

Like any other mass-media form (advertising, television, movies), pornography is a landscape pretty much exclusively inhabited by the young and the pretty. The surprising success of legendary porn director Joe Gage's *Dad Takes a Fishing Trip* and its follow-up *Dad Goes to College* both capitalized on the market for sexy daddy-boy narratives and kicked off a tsunami of imitations. It's gotten to the point where anyone with some hair on his chest can get labeled "daddy" when it comes to online porn. There is a tiny niche for geriatric porn as a specialty item, which is refreshing. But outside of hotoldermale.com, there's not much representation of aging in the realm of gay male porn. Without the visual modeling, it's hard to envision being sexual past 40, let alone past 60.

Roger had a life-changing experience at a Body Electric intensive retreat. Although he made a bunch of friends, people repeatedly referred to him as an elder. He hated and resented the term, because to him it means old and decrepit. We talked about reframing elderhood and the meaningful roles older men play in a community. At Burning Man, I saw a camp populated by elders who had hung out a welcoming banner that read "We Will Listen to You." Having occupied center-stage for the prime of their lives, elders can serve as audience for succeeding generations, admiring triumphs and making space for the inevitable woes and disappointments. The men's consciousness movement encourages elders to accept the responsibility of blessing younger men, which is a powerful gift that both parties need for healthy emotional and spiritual development. This is the subject of iconoclastic psychologist James Hillman's book *The Force of Character: And the Lasting Life*. "In later years," Hillman wrote, "feelings of altruism and kindness to strangers play a larger role, as if psychological and cultural factors redirect, even override, genetic inheritance and its aim of propagation."

All this was helpful and mind-expanding for Roger. Nevertheless, he related heavily when I mentioned that one of the obstacles to embracing elderhood is the feeling that you yourself did not receive sufficient blessing as a younger man. Especially if you're in a place of just now living your adolescence or youth by embracing your sexuality openly, you may not be ready to take your place as an elder.

Paradoxically, it may be the very absence of visual representation of older people that gives porn extra value as a fertile field for fantasy. Although there's a sweet validation that comes from mirroring (seeing people in porn who look like you do), without that mirroring the erotic imagination is free to run wild and project yourself onto the people in whatever porn you're watching. Toward the end of his life, behavioral psychologist B. F. Skinner argued that much of what we call aging is not an inexorable process of decline but a change in the physical and social environment. "As vision, hearing and taste fade, and erogenous tissues grow less sensitive, the elderly become bored, discouraged and depressed," he said. "They no longer receive powerful reinforcement from the environment, and fewer things seem worth doing." But that can be changed, he said. He specifically recommended that foods be more highly flavored, those who can't read listen to book recordings, and that "pornography can be used to extend sexuality into old age."

Gay novelist Andrew Holleran goes so far as to say that its value to elderly people is the best argument for pornography. "If pneumonia is considered 'the old person's friend' (because it carries you off), the same may be said of porn," Holleran wrote in an essay published in *The Gay and Lesbian Review*. "It lets you, at an advanced age, have sex with people you would never be able to in real life. In fact, it lets you have sex with people you could not have had sex with when you were young...without all the things that can go wrong during sex—smells, shit, disillusionment, erectile failure, a sudden wrong note that ruins things, the fact that the soufflé of Lust can collapse in a single unforeseen and irreversible instant."

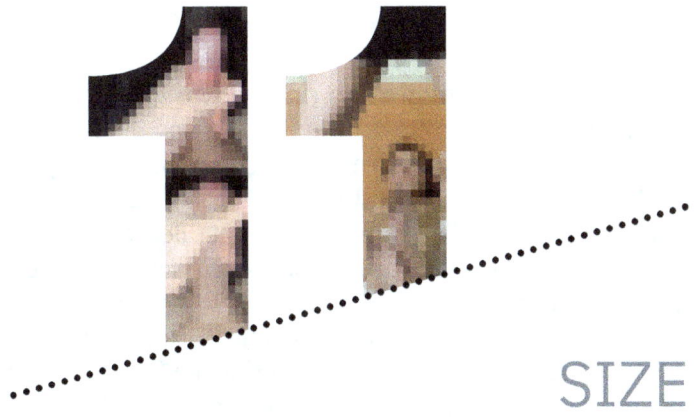

11 SIZE

Clark says poignantly, "I know they want my big dick, but do they want me?"

Howard tells me about a hot-and-heavy flirtation that becomes anxious-making when the flirty texting proceeds to "show me your dick" or "come over and fuck me with your big dick" — because the dick in question is decidedly smaller than average.

For Mario, a Mexican-American composer in his mid-thirties, there's a very complicated relationship between pornography and his experience of his own body. "I am in recovery for sexual compulsion, which is in remission now thanks to therapy and working the 12 steps," he told me. "Prior to program, I would spend most weekends glued to the computer, sniffing poppers and smoking pot and masturbating to porn nonstop. Because I have issues with my penis size (its length is on the shorter end of average, but the girth is below), I used porn to engage in destructive, shameful comparing and despairing. I would eroticize that by masturbating to a picture of someone I believed was superior to me and had more power than me."

Like many gay men, Mario grew up without proper mentorship or role models. His father was gay and stayed in the closet until Mario was 19. Even after coming out, he was so riddled with internalized homophobia that he was unable to be any sort of positive older male figure in his son's life. On top of that, Mario hit puberty and eventually came out right in the midst of the AIDS crisis, which instilled the notion that sex was dangerous and deadly. This combination of factors left him especially susceptible to turning to porn to teach him about his sexuality. "I think I placed expectations on porn that it could never fulfill. I want porn to be more 'realistic' and show different kinds of bodies. I want to see men with smaller cocks. I know it's weird, but if I see someone or something being objectified sexually, I suddenly see it validated. And by extension, if I don't share that quality, it invalidates me."

Porn did help tremendously just by validating his sexual desires. "I have such shame admitting I find a man hot or I would want to engage in some sort of sexual activity with a hot man. Admiring and being turned on by a penis (which statistically speaking is very, very likely to be larger than mine) is a challenge. I try to let myself say yes to that attraction and normalize it."

After abstaining from pornography for four years, he recently dipped back into it again and found his relationship to it has changed. For one thing, he spends less time on it (and more time on Facebook). "I still don't have a positive paradigm for viewing my genitals in a way that allows me to feel sexy and hot, even though I have a boyfriend who finds me super attractive and I get tons of validation from men, especially at clothing-optional events or sex parties. I'm getting better at learning to appreciate other men's genitals and manage to not put myself down in the process, but it's not easy. Hookup culture requires me to take pictures of myself naked to share with potential partners, and I think it creates a larger pressure in my mind to measure up to a porn-star standard in order to be seen as desirable."

* * *

Paradox: the more porn I look at, the smaller I think my dick is.

The 12-step motto "Compare and despair" is never truer than when it comes to men and the size of their dicks. In the healthiest situations, men are exposed at an early age to a range of other men's bodies — in family bathing contexts, changing rooms at swimming pools and beaches, Phys Ed classes in school, locker rooms at gyms. With time and experience, most guys eventually come to understand the distinction between a grow-er and a show-er. Some dicks that are tiny when flaccid fill out surprisingly when engorged; many dicks that look dangly in the locker room don't get that much longer when the guy has an erection. It's easy to be philosophical about size when your dick is average; it's much harder when your dick is smaller than average. Men who have smaller than average dicks tend to obsess about length and girth more than other men. But even that perception can be distorted by overexposure to pornography and underexposure to real-life penises, which is a major unfortunate consequence of the trend in American schools away from mandatory gym classes, showering, and group nudity.

An article in the legendary leathersex magazine *Drummer* by an author calling himself Fledermaus articulates a variation on the grower/shower dichotomy. "Cocks come in a great range of shapes and sizes," he

writes. "One basic difference, which you rarely see discussed in any of our literature, is that between what are often called 'blood cocks' and 'meat cocks.' Blood cocks are quite small when flaccid and expand greatly as the corpora cavernosa fill with blood. Meat cocks remain relatively large even when flaccid and generally do not change length greatly when they become hard." The classic example of a blood cock is Michelangelo's David (or any other Renaissance reference to Greek or Roman sculpture). For a meat cock — well, look at any porn model. The article notes that both types of cocks have the potential to be equally large when erect, but meat cocks get more attention.

For the record: in 2015 British investigators reviewed 17 published studies that included more than 15,500 men whose penises were measured by health professionals using a standard procedure. The average length of a flaccid penis was 3.6 inches, the average length of a flaccid stretched penis was 5.3

inches, and the average length of an erect penis was 5.2 inches. The average circumference of a flaccid penis was 3.7 inches, and the average circumference of an erect penis was 4.6 inches.

"While most models are presented in poses that make them appear to be massive brutes, most of them are really, really short. There's a reason for it," John Preston once wrote. "While gay male mythology makes a great deal of noise about various cock sizes and the ways you're supposed to be able to discern them — big feet, big ears, et al — the truth is that most dicks are about the same length and width. There are variations but, for the most part, the differences between various dicks are slight. Thus, if you have a perfectly average penis on a very short man, it looks huge. Put the same cock on a very tall man, and it will look small. The munchkins win out in the model sweepstake. Knowing all this makes it difficult to believe that the mean-looking biker on the cover of *Drummer* is really anything more than a gym bunny who stands only as tall as my tits."

Porn has been a mixed blessing for my client Jeremy, whose self-consciousness about his dick size has plagued him his entire adult life, often to the point of paralysis. He has had a fair share of mutually enjoyable sex with casual partners and long-time boyfriends. He is a slim, attractive middle-aged man with, I can say with professional authority, a completely average-sized cock. Yet he judges himself as insufficiently masculine because of the size of his dick. He thinks it looks like the penis of a child rather than that of a grown man. The prospect of anal sex brings up his negative feelings about his dick. "I would like to fuck someone but I won't because I can't because I have a small dick and I can't make any impact." He had a bad experience shopping for condoms that felt snug enough, and it was demoralizing, and now he's so freaked out he won't try it again. His ideas about adult masculinity come partly from viewing other men cruising for sex in the sauna at his health club but mostly, of course, from looking at pornography. Jerking off to porn constitutes 99% of his sex life nowadays. Ironically, the emergence in recent years of bear porn has provided a healing refuge. Always drawn to homemade rather than commercial porn, it gratifies him to witness sexual interaction between regular-looking guys whose bellies are so big that their dicks look tiny.

Larson came to see me because, as he put it. "I want to learn to love my dick better." He wrote me a poignantly articulate e-mail saying, "I've always been insecure about my small, hairy and very thin penis. I've tried to overcome it over the years by putting myself out there in naked situations and talking to some guys about it. Sometimes I feel better about it than others, but the feeling of shame and embarrassment when I take off my pants in front of another guy never fully goes away. A few times I've been dating a guy and everything seems to be going well, but then he loses interest after getting naked for the first time. This happened to me recently, and the guy examined my dick in such a way that made it pretty clear he was disappointed. It really has me triggered. I want to enjoy a healthy sex life but I'm nervous to let anyone know what's between my legs. I know it's not my fault and it's just how I was born, but I just can't seem to get over it and accept it."

I am aware that many, possibly most men live with a certain amount of anxiety and self-consciousness about the size of their dicks. I chalk it up largely to the ubiquity of online porn in our lives, which virtually never shows dicks that aren't large and hard. (The models may be 4'10", as John Preston suggested, but how would you know?) I'm also aware that having a smaller-than-average dick can cause crippling anxiety for men. I would say that there are three aspects to this situation: mental (how you think about yourself and your body), verbal (how you talk about yourself and your body to other guys), and physical (what you do with your body). In all of these realms, the challenge is to integrate your genitals into the rest of your being, to see and feel and present your dick as part of the whole you rather than a split-off or problematic entity unto itself. Easier said than done, I know. But if you have a small dick that works — that is, it gets hard, it feels good, it squirts — you're better off than plenty of guys with bigger dicks that don't necessarily get hard or function pleasurably.

Although it's easy to assume that "everyone" prizes and prefers big dicks, the bigger the better, in my experience that's not actually true. We may admire big dicks in porn the way we admire handsome Hollywood actors, but anyone with any common sense realizes that love and sex and pleasure come in all sizes and shapes. Depending on what kind of sex you enjoy, there are plenty of guys who prefer smaller dicks to larger ones, and plenty of guys for whom the person attached to the dick is way more important than what the dick looks like.

Larson turns out to be a sweet, friendly, cute 30-something fellow who commutes between Toronto and Jersey City for work. Because of his anxiety about getting naked with other guys, he's been having trouble getting and staying hard. He had more than one relationship in which there was mutual attraction, great chemistry, and no self-consciousness. He knows he has features that other people like: handsome face, nice butt, hairy body. He'd like to be able to say, "I don't care, I love my dick." The reality is that he doesn't like how his dick looks. "If I met someone with my dick, I'd be disappointed."

He gets his ideas of what dicks are supposed to look like from porn, naturally. In school he was too nervous to look at other guys' dicks when changing in the locker room, so the first dicks he saw were the ones he glimpsed in gay porn between the ages of 10 and 20. "On the internet, dicks are all big and juicy and thick." He had a serious boyfriend in college who had "a huge dick," which reinforced his porn-influenced perception of the average dick size. They had great sex and were "totally in love," so when they broke up, Larson was heartbroken for a year. He moved to San Francisco at age 25 and started meeting guys on Craigslist. He loved going to Kabuki, a Japanese-style public bathhouse popular with gay men. It was a healing environment for him. In nude environments, it makes him happy to see little dicks.

Since moving to the East Coast, his confidence has taken a dive. With casual hookups, he feels a lot of anxiety and has difficulty staying hard. He doesn't know what to do the first time. "Some guys won't go down on you unless you're hard." The last guy actually held out his fingers to measure the size of Larson's dick. In chat rooms he will sometimes interact with someone who will tease him about his dick in a way that is perversely hot, though it's tricky – there's a fine line between submissiveness and being insulted. In lieu of steady sex partners, he looks at porn every day, spending 15 minutes to two hours looking at Tumblr blogs devoted to male nudists, regular guys, and fuck porn.

With guys like Larson, I always think it's a good idea to step back and look at the big picture. We live in a culture inundated with porn with all its excitement and distortions, and hookup sex induces the illusion that everyone is or should be available for all sex all the time right away, which causes more anxiety than pleasure. I encouraged him to check out more casual nudist environments and to scale back looking at porn. It's asking a lot to expect someone to stop completely, but as with any habit you're trying to shake, it helps to bring mindfulness to the situation. One method I've found useful is to keep a log of how long you spend looking at porn, what you look at, what turns you on, and what makes you feel bad about yourself.

Most of all, I suggested to Larson, he needs to develop a rap to share with guys before meeting them to hookup. Having a smaller-than-average dick is one of those conditions that it's probably wise to have a conversation about with potential partners before the pants come off, like HIV status or medical conditions or foreskin anomalies. It may be embarrassing to talk about, but it can also be a catalyst to intimacy and charm. My experience is that if you accept yourself, other people will accept you as well, and if not, well, fuck 'em. Or more to the point, don't fuck 'em.

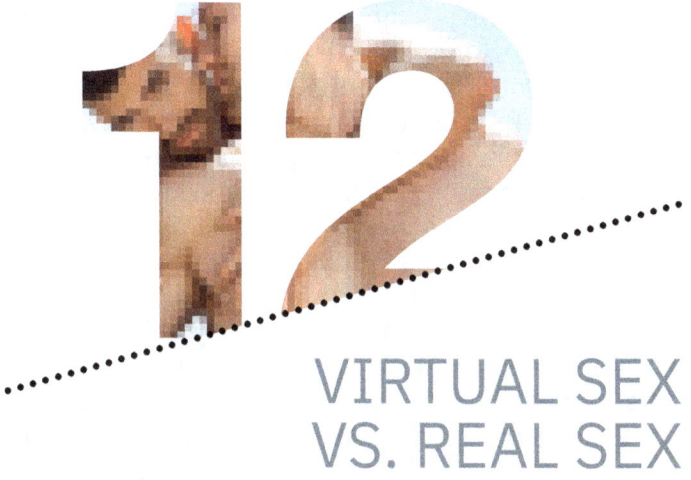

12
VIRTUAL SEX VS. REAL SEX

Here's a perfect example of the paradox of porn: the internet has made it possible for men who are closeted or socially anxious or who live in isolated rural areas to seek out information about gay life safely, in privacy, and at their own pace. Online cruising sites and social media apps facilitate making contact with other men with similar tastes and interests near where you live.

But organizing a hookup or even a simple coffee date online is one thing. Conducting a conversation and negotiating a social encounter with another man is something else entirely, and porn is not very helpful with that.

Gino is a 60-something-year-old technician who works in broadcasting. He called me in a crisis. He has no love in his life and he wants that but he believes his life is over. He has been having fits of hysterical crying. He's a highly anxious gay man who's been in the closet all his life. He's had tons of sex with strangers, but he's never been able to sustain a relationship and never told anyone in his family or at work that he's gay. He is a rapid ejaculator and during sex he often gets so worried that he won't satisfy his partners that he can't get it up at all. He watches a lot of porn and has all the misconceptions that come from that: Everybody else is having a lot of sex, but me. I should be able to get hard and fuck for hours. (He really thought he was the only guy who struggles with rapid ejaculation.)

I suggested that he's underpracticed at getting to know someone and exploring intimacy. He can't tell the difference between going on a date and making a marriage proposal. That's how unsocialized and inexperienced he is. But he's extremely well-practiced at going on SilverDaddies.com and connecting with guys who are his type (younger non-white dudes who like to have sex with older white dudes). Case in point: last night Rani came over, a chunky kid who's 35 or so, half Kuwaiti, half Italian. He's friendly and smart and warm, and Gino would like to see him again but hardly knows how to proceed. I had him imagine his way through 10 possible things he'd like to do with Rani besides fuck, and it didn't take too much effort for him to come up with:

1. have dinner
2. go to a movie or a play or a museum
3. take a ride to the country
4. sit and visit at home
5. watch TV
6. go to the beach and swim
7. go kayaking with a gay outdoors group
8. go to the Bronx Botanical Garden
9. take a hike
10. work out together (bicycle, weights)

For Gino, it's hard to believe that inviting someone to do one of these things isn't leading him on or proposing marriage.

Sean is about the same age as Gino and only started exploring his attraction to men at the age of 60. His life circumstances are more constricted — he's been married to a woman his entire adult life, they run the family business selling antique furniture, and their three grown children still live at home with them in suburban Boston. For him, social media has opened up an entire new world of both imagination and experience. When he first got online, he would spend all day clicking and chatting with other closeted married guys in a Yahoo group. He's scaled that back to an hour or less each day. With his wife's wary approval, he has formed an ongoing sexual friendship with Dylan, a closeted single guy who lives in Portland, Maine. They talk on the phone every day and meet once a month for an overnight tryst at a hotel halfway between them.

Perhaps because he's the oldest in a large Irish-Catholic brood, Sean has a gregarious personality and a gift for care-giving. He's sufficiently socialized that he's doesn't look to porn for cues on how to maneuver his way through the gay world. So although his gay life is cordoned off from his straight life, he has developed a wide network of friends via social media to whom he sends daily text messages. They exchange sexy pictures (Sean likes looking at butts) and sometimes conduct webcam sessions, but he isn't in it for cybersex. He deletes most of the pictures his buddies send him, but since he knows that Dylan likes redheads, he forwards handsome ginger pix to him. He likes looking at tender action scenes in porn, not rough stuff. When I ask what he has learned from porn, he said it alerted him to how guys get turned on being touched in certain places (nipples, perineum) that are not especially erotic to him. He has casual sexual encounters with plenty of men, perhaps because he's mature enough that rejection doesn't stop him in his tracks. He doesn't take it personally. In fact, I would say he makes out like a bandit, more than plenty of available gay men half his age.

Fred is another sexual late bloomer for whom cruising apps became a doorway into a wonderland of GPS-enabled hookups. But then he became obsessed, addicted to the ego-gratification of messages from guys cruising him, excited to hear the little sound that goes with a new message appearing in your mailbox, the flash on the home screen of your phone when a push notification says you've received a message or a woof or a grope or a wink from Scruff or Manhunt. He found himself at professional social occasions excusing himself to go to the bathroom to check his messages from Grindr.

He's quite clear about the corrosive aspect of the apps. "An ugly fat person writes to me. I don't answer and then feel bad. Someone thinks I'm fat and ugly, they block me, and I'm furious. They like my cock but when I send a face pic I never hear from them again." In some ways he sees GPS-oriented apps as honest, fine, democratic, win some lose some…but then he encounters pic collectors. And he gets lost in time and misses important events – a friend's film premiere, another friend's birthday party. Even while on the phone with his career coach, he was checking Grindr. That's when he realized he was out of control. He deleted them all at once. He's experiencing withdrawal big-time: edginess, fear, loneliness, exhaustion, sadness. He feels like Grindr drove him to do dangerous things, like hook up with someone who lived at the end of a dirt road in rural Connecticut. The encounter sounded quite lovely to me — they rimmed, fingered, sucked, fucked, then dozed off, then the guy made Fred dinner — but Fred didn't know if he was there by choice or by compulsion. This was all about thrill, adventure, the unknown, being a hunter in the jungle, being independent, masculine, powerful, rich, brave, sexy, free. The next day he wanted it all over again with the same guy, who wasn't available. So Fred went on to other guys, not so satisfying. He knows that his compulsive sex-hunting is an attempt to soothe his anxiety and his loneliness. Sometimes that works. Sometimes it only makes things worse.

When someone repeatedly returns to the same unsatisfying behavior, rather than labeling this impulse insanity or neurosis or addiction, I try to determine what positive choice is being made. What need is insistently trying to be met? Only when I understand that can we start to imagine if there's a healthier or more satisfying way to meet that need. For example, it's obvious that overeating has an emotional component. No amount of food can satiate a hunger for love, attention, self-esteem, or relief from sadness. Similarly, compulsive cruising for sex and jerking off to porn can be attempts to relieve stress and anxiety by discharging nervous energy; it can be driven by loneliness and a desire to connect; it can be displacement activity when you're avoiding something that you're scared or reluctant to do; it can be a purely self-indulgent and/or well-deserved reward in the middle of a life bristling with demands and attending to other people's needs. It takes wisdom, courage, and often support to identify the deeper emotional craving that porn-watching seeks to satisfy.

For Fred, whose work involves large projects that take years to complete, it seems clear that his porn-watching and sex-hunting are efforts to grant himself short-term treats to get him through the long haul. A key inquiry for him became: What are some reliable

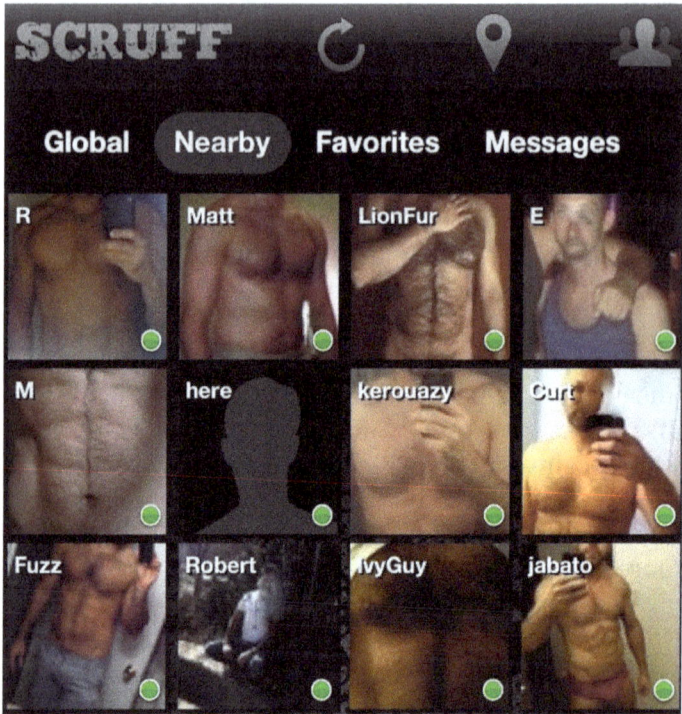

treats that are healthy? Practicing piano, playing with his cat, working in the garden, meditating, drinking tea. Those are sweet and fun, but they lack the element of adventure and connection that are also important to Fred. Therapy has helped him recognize that it's no longer true that he's sexually deprived. He's had plenty of sex. He needs to rewrite that story.

Conor continues to struggle with shame around the prospect of disclosing his HIV-positive status to potential sex partners. Although it's increasingly common for men to be upfront in their profiles, even using (+) as part of their handles, Conor has been reluctant to do that and on several apps has chosen to let the impression stand that he's HIV-negative. As we talked about it during one therapy session, he decided to delete his Manhunt and Adam4Adam profiles on the spot and immediately felt relief, because they were a waste of time and yielded nothing. Most guys he hooks up with he meets on Grindr. I had him tell me what was good and bad about Grindr for him. He noted that it's good for making friends in the neighborhood and meeting potential dates (two guys he met on Grindr have become ongoing friends), and it can be an entertaining way to pass the time. On the down side, he's aware that, entertaining as it may be, Grindr can also be "a total time-waster" that enables procrastination. "I keep checking it off and on all evening. Alerts keep me engaged in conversations that are inconsequential. And I can't say no I when someone wants a blowjob."

It's not coincidental that so many of the mixed feelings we have about pornography also apply to technology and social media. The mobile devices that have become attached to us like anatomical appendages provide convenience when it comes to seeking information and making connection. At the same time they're equally good at providing distraction and helping us avoid direct human contact. And those qualities get fiendishly amplified when the shiny pleasures of sex get involved.

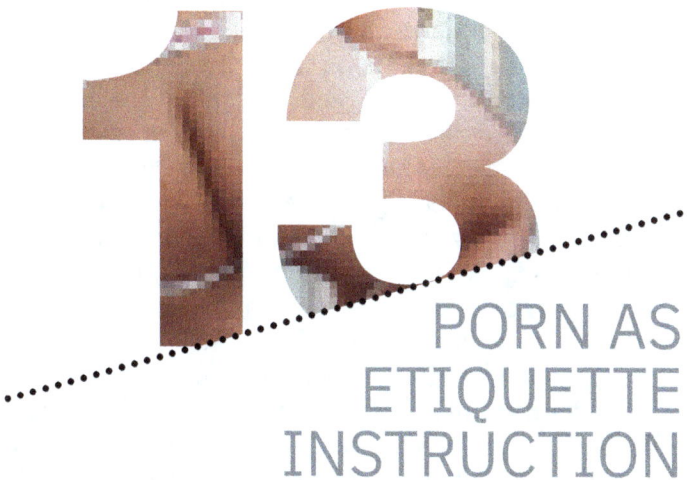

13

PORN AS ETIQUETTE INSTRUCTION

Paradox: when you're young or inexperienced, it's thrilling to discover porn in any format that gives you a peek at gay sex and how it works. It's life-changing to watch other people interact sexually and to feel your own feelings looking at hot guys and different sex acts. Learning what turns you on is an important piece of sexual education and development. BUT porn only shows sexual interaction, with minimal or negligible social, emotional, cultural or geographical context, which has the unintended consequence of teaching guys to sexualize ALL emotions, ALL interactions. If he says "hello" to me, does that mean he wants to fuck me? If I shake his hand at a party, does that mean I've agreed to have sex with him? If not fucking, what happens after "hello"? A friend told me about arranging a hookup online. When the guy arrived, my friend opened the door, and the next thing he knew, before a word was spoken, the guy had his tongue in my friend's mouth. Apparently Ding-Dong Boy hadn't even learned to say "hello."

Before the internet, before ubiquitous online pornography, if you wanted to learn about gay life and you didn't have much access to social opportunities or were too shy to go to bars or clubs or meetings or gay events, you could always read books and magazines. There is a distinguished literary tradition of gay novels that have given generations of gay men ideas about how our tribe meets, greets, falls in love, fumbles, works, plays, laughs, cries, mourns, and deals with the life issues we all face (our parents, our families, our spiritual questions, our bodies). We live in an era now, though, where it's difficult to muster the energy, attention span, patience, and willpower to sit down and read a book like E.M. Forster's *Maurice* or Andrew Holleran's *Dancer from the Dance* or Neil Bartlett's *Ready to Catch Him Should He Fall* or one of E. Lynn Harris's pulpy romances that might offer some glimpse of how gay men relate to each other socially and emotionally as well as sexually. The ground-breaking British television series *Queer as Folk* (1999-2000) provided that service for a much wider audience, as did its American remake and the more recent HBO series *Looking*.

I'm at a gay wedding in the Catskills where one of the grooms and many of the guests are psychotherapists. One therapist at my table says, "It's so unusual being in a group of gay men who are so open and friendly, where people you don't know will come up and talk to you. I've been to gay bars where I've said hi and offered my hand to shake, and they turned and walked away without saying anything." I was appalled and surprised — it's not my experience of gay social life, but others have told similar stories of being rudely rebuffed attempting to make contact or conversation in bars.

It's always been difficult to penetrate the mystery of socializing in gay bars, conquering social anxiety, combating the presumption that everybody else knows everybody else and I alone am the unwelcome intruder. But our contemporary social media technology has only exacerbated the problem. We're so used to communicating via devices that we've forgotten or never learned the social skills required to meet someone face-to-face with a modicum of graciousness, friendliness, simple respect. We communicate with our friends in tiny bursts of text-message shorthand. And the strangers we cruise on social-media smartphone apps are not quite flesh-and-blood creatures to us, they're just funny little squares on our phones, often passing in front of our eyes without heads or shirts or pants.

Pornography has a role to play in this as well. One of the paradoxes of gay male porn is that it shows all the juicy explicit details of sexual intimacy while rarely giving the slightest hint of emotional or social intimacy. What do people say in order to meet the people they have sex with? How do they negotiate the sex they have? What happens after everybody orgasms? It's hard to tell because you rarely see those interactions. So guys who watch a lot of porn — especially younger guys, guys who are in the closet, late bloomers, and the sexually inexperienced — can get lulled into thinking that's all there is and forget (or never learn) how to conduct the simplest forms of interpersonal socializing. Because if you've never seen it, how are you supposed to know what it looks like?

Steve McQueen's film *Shame* captures this contemporary phenomenon with scrupulous specificity. The main character, an apparently hard-working and successful businessman played by Michael Fassbender, devotes virtually all of his leisure time to communing with porn on his laptop, which he navigates with the intensity and efficiency of an astronaut. The images and scenarios that flood his brain enable him to negotiate wordless trysts with women he meets on the subway or men he encounters at late-night sex clubs. The one time he finds himself agreeing to have dinner with an attractive co-worker, his awkward attempts to chat her up and the increasingly gaping pauses in the conversation result in the most excruciating date scene I've ever seen in a movie.

If you've sexualized all social needs and interactions, then perhaps it makes sense that saying "hello" to a stranger means "I want to fuck you." And if you say "hello" back, that means, "Okay, you can fuck me." And if you don't want that, then you just don't say anything. But that's not how a functional social life works.

Ryan wants "something between a husband and a hookup." He craves a sense of intimacy and connectedness over time that doesn't necessarily mean making an exclusive commitment or taking the express lane to domestic partnership. The middle ground is surprisingly difficult to navigate. He met someone on Grindr while staying with friends on Fire Island. He and his hookup were having a great time so they drifted into making out, having sex, and talking for three hours instead of going to a party. Later Ryan got yelled at by his hosts: "Three hours? *Three hours?!?* Pines hookups are 15 minutes!"

The video "Handsome Man" by gay singer-songwriter Matt Alber represents an antidote or companion to a steady diet of porn. In just 4 minutes and 44 seconds, it captures a multitude of glimpses of gay male intimacy that hardly ever show up even in full-length films and TV shows about gay life.

Two good-looking guys who aren't kids, who have facial hair, geeky glasses, and imperfect bodies — 39-year-old Alber and his buddy Alan — wake up in bed together. They get up slowly, nuzzling and smooching. They have breakfast, they go back to bed, they take pictures of each other. They share a book. One writes a secret note on the back of a strip of photo-booth shots they'd obviously taken recently. The other one reads it after the guy leaves, and you see emotion surge into his eyes.

As these scenes play out, we hear the song "Handsome Man," which kicks off Alber's EP *Wind Sand Stars*. The lyric conveys some of the simple thoughts and questions that emerge when you're Getting to Know Someone:

Hey handsome man what'd ya do last night?
Did you have a good time?
Was the music all right?
Did you wear that jacket with the deep blue jeans?
Bet the boys went crazy, bet you caused a scene.
Cuz everybody smiles when a
handsome man walks by...

Say handsome man, where you off to now?
Are you out in the garden or off to town?
Are there any new songs that you're listening to?
I'm gonna take ya dancing when I come to see you...

Handsome man, can I ask you this?
I know we've both been loved
and we've both been kissed
But when the hounds are sleeping
and the night is deep
Will you tell me the story of you and me?

I love that Matt Alber prizes these tiny mundane touches of gay male affection and interest and that he's willing to model them, to be a kind of teacher of gay intimacy. I would love to see more gay artists create scenes like that rather than leave the teaching of sex and intimacy to porn, which never set out to do that in the first place.

14

WILD SEX

As a sex therapist and couples counselor, I spend a fair amount of time helping people figure out how to have sex that is more intimate, connected, and emotionally fulfilling, on the assumption that it's what they want and it's what makes sex satisfying. At the same time, I can't ignore the reality that not every gay man wants loving domestic-partner sex every time. I don't. There are times when nothing is more satisfying than raunchy erotic rough-housing in a dark place with someone whose name you don't know whom you'll never see again — and anyone else who wants to join. Sometimes what is fun is simply to surrender to the animal physicality of male sexuality. The tribal connection. The joy of tapping into the transpersonal essence of sexual flow that has nothing to do with chakras or eye-gazing or commitment. Maybe the pleasure includes some deep edgy experience of spiritual communion — merging with infinity, or the endless chain of life, of being born and dying, reveling in the body functions that go with being alive. And maybe it goes beyond any rational conscious thought.

This is the mythological realm of Pan, who rules in dead silence in the middle of the night, when men roam parks and forests and backroom bars hungry for a visceral experience that departs from daylight social contact.

When 9/11 happened, my first instinct was to go to Central Park the next day and find some guy to blow in the bushes — and I did. When a blackout spread throughout the East Coast, I rode my bike to the Rambles and joined the scrum of men wandering around in the dark, in silence, dropping our pants, dropping to our knees, letting our asses hang out, communing in the way that men have communed in the wild forever. Not unlike Tobias Schneebaum's stories of hanging out with natives along the Amazon who went on raids, killed a member of a rival tribe, tore out his heart, cooked it and ate it, then took turns fucking each other in the ass. This isn't hearts and flowers. This is pandemonium. This is showing up at The Cock in the East Village a little after midnight, when the club is pretty sparse, drinking a couple of vodka tonics to get a buzz on while the room fills up, and then releasing into the shoulder-to-shoulder press, waiting for a hard cock to emerge from somebody's trousers, then getting on your knees and pleasuring it while he makes out with someone up above, who takes his dick out, so you go back and forth, and a crowd gathers, and you're working your way around a circle with your expert hot mouth, servicing one hard cock after another, occasionally getting a juicy reward in your mouth, sometimes accepting the offer of a hit of poppers, merging with the moment of gay male empowered sexuality, in the dark, late at night. A couple of hours go by and you're on your feet again, heading out to hail a taxi, and you notice that your pants are filthy from the knees down. And you reel a little bit from the gap between outside and inside, the polite society of traffic lights and New York City cabdrivers distinct from the collective surge of energy inside the sleazy gay bar.

Other contexts for non-heartful sex:
- Invitation-only hotel-room gatherings organized by and for closeted married men to blow off steam with kindred spirits at lunchtime or after-work before heading home;
- Sleazy leather bars where it's not unusual for guys to blow each other standing at the bar or in the men's room (under the influence — one reason to get loaded is to surrender conscious resistance/reluctance);
- Quick-n-dirty businessman blowjobs (on his way to get a haircut, Brendan stops by for a three-minute quickie, whipping just his dick out of his snazzy suit);
- Groups as live porn;
- BDSM rough-sex scenarios that are less about pleasure, connection, and orgasm than about masculine initiation, submitting to a trusted authority, enduring an ordeal (cf. Bound Gods' "Bound in Public" series);
- Gym sex in the sauna or steam room — another form of athletic prowess, mutual admiration, masculine communing, surrender of identity (no clothes, no labels), voyeurism and exhibitionism, lurking and leading, titillation and transgressiveness;
- Drug-fuelled sex parties — riding the edge of chemically induced merger.

These images are clearly deep and mythological, and in some way they drive the fantasies that show up again and again in gay male porn. Instant access, limitless availability, powerful masculine sensuality, the potent shame-driven cycle of control-and-release, the onslaught of smell and touch, rough and tender, slippery and hard, tastes that are sweet and bitter — variations on poet Mary Oliver's aperçu about "the eagerness to be wild and perfect for a moment, before [we] are nothing, forever."

* * *

Then there is the paradox that pleasure taken to excess becomes its opposite. You get numbed out, disgusted by pornsex. My friend Tim inherited his friend Nelson's estate, including his apartment, his music collection (thousands of CDs), and his gargantuan stash of porn, which included several outdated external hard drives stuffed with images downloaded from the early days of the internet as well as large boxes of VHS tapes and DVDs. I agreed to take off his hands the box of DVDs, strictly for research purposes. My husband and I spent an hour one afternoon cataloguing the contents, and we experienced the curious cycle familiar to porn aficionados.

At first, you're completely excited. What could be more exhilarating than watching people fuck? As we go through the box and read off the titles, our excitement diminishes. The titles sound ridiculous. The cheesy covers blur together and become one generic cheap skin flick. I witness firsthand the strange combination of joy and joylessness that infects any compulsive collector, whether the treasured objects are coins, stamps, autographs, comic books, record albums, or porn. You're past savoring, past making choices. You can't stop. You're in the dangerous realm that ancient Roman philosopher Epicurus warned about. Although he famously declared that pleasure is the greatest happiness in life, he didn't mean hedonism, endless sensual indulgence. Epicurus counseled that the greatest pleasure was "having enough" and cautioned against indulging pleasures that only leave you wanting more, like a thirst for fame or money. What would he have made of internet porn? Actually, he was pretty prescient about it. Sex for him fell in the category of pleasures that can never be satisfied. He ranked it below the supreme pleasure of friendship.

Sorting through Nelson's collection, I pick a few videos I'm curious to look at and possibly take with me on a writing retreat as "field research." From the unboxed discs on a spindle, I pick four and run them through the Blu-Ray player. They're all from Hot Desert Knights, a company that made a lot of early bareback videos with a big disclaimer upfront urging guys who are HIV-negative to do everything they can to stay that way. First I watch *Birthday Fuck Party*, in which a guy named Kenboy celebrates his 28th (ha) birthday party in a sling getting serially fucked. The guys are not especially attractive: quite clearly HIV-positive (facial wasting), quite possibly tweaking (glassy-eyed). I'm turned on watching guys with boners line up to fuck the same guy, and I realize that's the moment I'm waiting for, when one guy stops fucking (whether he's cum or not) and the next guy steps up to fuck the same guy. But the quality is terrible. The aesthete in me starts critiquing the video as art, which is a buzz-kill. Then I start feeling sorry for the guys, who look like they're in some overlit, sweaty, overheated, drug-entranced circle of hell. I turn the sound down, starting to feel concerned that my neighbors might hear the generic porn grunting. Then I start feeling a little ashamed of watching this crap.

Much the same arc happens looking at *Barebacking With Jeff Palmer #3: Gang Fucked*. The opening montage previews all the scenes, which take place in a bare room with the star (a smooth-skinned Middle American 30-ish white boy with the goofy grin of a depraved cherub) lying on a cushioned footrest getting fucked fore and aft. The concept of group action excites me but the guys are unattractive, and I can't stand watching the action scenes for more than a couple of minutes. *Berlin Raunch* is even worse, just five two-person scenes with a dead soundtrack.

I slide a Treasure Island Media disc called *Deeper* into my external hard drive and let my Mac convert the .avi file into something it can view. I believe it's the sequel to *Dawson's 20 Load Weekend*, which I've seen before. Watching *Deeper* is a revelation after the other crappy porn videos I sampled. It's one of the masterpieces of Treasure Island Media, another company that specializes in unscripted bareback orgy scenes, though with higher production values than most porn producers. Shot over five different dates in 2006 with many of the same participants, it features Dawson (a handsome, sexy, balding white hunk who's not starlet young, probably mid-to-late 30s) first in a hotel room getting fucked by as many guys as possible and then in some kind of bar venue getting occasionally fucked but mostly sucking cocks and taking loads on his tongue and on his face. There's a felch-hound who follows him around licking the cum out of his ass or off his face and feeding it back to him. The group action is steady and hot, the dicks are pretty sexy and functional, and Dawson's tireless and shame-free cock/cum-hunger is riveting to observe.

The part that really turns me on, though, comes at the end of the movie. After a long session of taking cocks and cum, tired and sweaty but insatiable Dawson takes a cameraman to a sex club called Folsom Gulch where he proceeds to get fucked through a gloryhole by

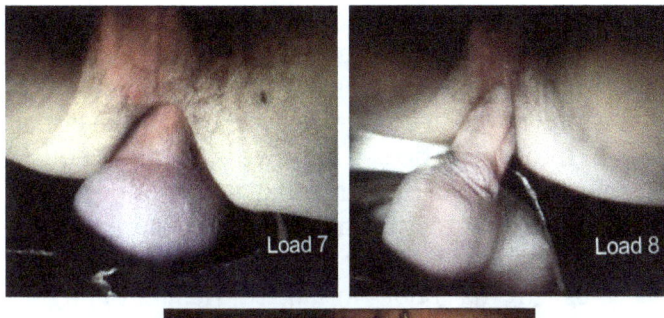

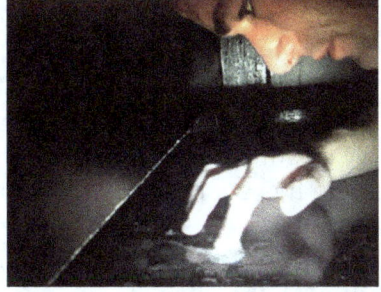

anyone who steps up, which turns out to be a total of eight guys. As with *Dawson's 20-Load Weekend*, Treasure Island Media flashes a title on the screen tallying the star's semen intake ("Load 7," "Load 8"). At the gloryhole they don't usually pull out and shoot on his ass, the cum definitely gets delivered deep inside him, and every time the title comes up, I get a little more turned on.

In contrast to the staged narratives concocted by Joe Gage (another high-quality gay porn auteur), these marathon sex videos are an erotic version of extreme-sports reality TV — sort of horrifying, sort of thrilling, tapping some mysterious element of riskiness and animality that pulls me in. I'm not high or drunk while watching the movie. I'm sitting at my desk letting it play while reading email and Facebook and waiting for my next client. But I could also imagine getting high and snorting poppers and disappearing into merging energetically with Dawson. There is a kind of transcendence and oblivion in his rapacious bottoming that taps some deep homosexual craving, to give and/or receive multiple packets of masculine essence in an ecstatic setting that is simultaneously transpersonal and dehumanized. It's a distant debased echo of temple prostitution, shamanic ceremonies, or the kind of tribal fertility rituals Gilbert Herdt describes in his book *Ritualized Homosexuality in Melanesia*. I suppose this is a perfect example of how porn-watching is so personal and private. The communion is nothing like watching a movie in a movie theater and sharing the group catharsis. It is an unquantifiably private experience.

Anyone who has spent time in an uninterrupted porn trance knows this cycle of engagement, excitement, leveling off, boredom, disenchantment, disgust, withdrawal, then back to re-engagement. The cycle can recur repeatedly in one session. It can manifest in patterns of binging and abstaining. And it can characterize a lifetime of looking at porn. For most gay men, the reality is that there are periods of time when porn is extremely important, fulfilling, empowering, and activating, and then there are times when it's not. Sometimes you lose your taste forever. Sometimes you come to it late, with the zeal of making up for lost time. As with books, music, food, and other pleasures, some people never lose their loyalty to the first beloved images from porn. For others, tastes morph over time and circumstance. What years ago — or was it minutes ago? — seemed unutterably hot now looks faintly ridiculous or merely quaint.

When you look back, sometimes it's with repulsion or embarrassment — "I can't believe that used to turn me on" — and sometimes with the fond nostalgia of uncovering youthful artifacts. Porn has a dynamic relationship with the highly individual museum of sexual fantasies we carry around in our psyches.

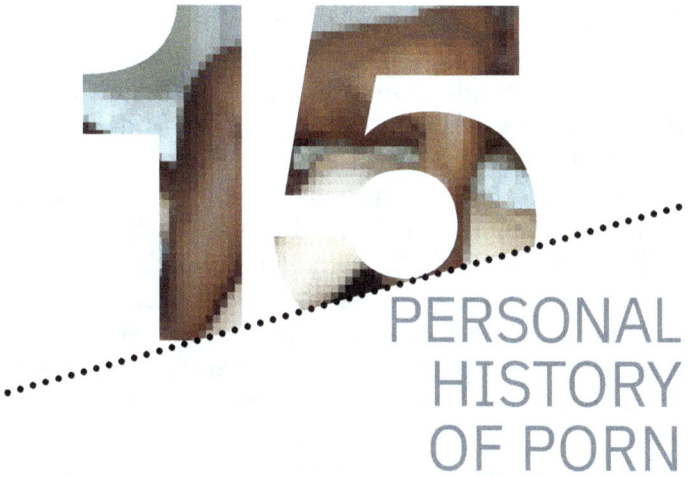

15 PERSONAL HISTORY OF PORN

It's almost impossible to be rational about pornography. Whatever I think about it, theorize about it, criticize about it, or celebrate about it co-exists with my actual consumption of porn, what I gaze upon at the end of the day, scrolling through my Tumblr blog for a little homoerotic entertainment before going to sleep. I'm convinced that almost every grown man who has access to the internet looks at porn every once in a while, if not every day. I'm pretty sure almost every gay man has a relationship to porn.

If you were looking over my shoulder, what would you see, and what would it tell you about me? You might get a glimpse of my taste in men or my taste in sexual activities from the pictures I linger over, the pictures I save to my iPad's photo gallery, the videos I click on to watch in full, the blogs I choose to "follow," the blog-posters whose websites or blogs I decide to examine further. But you can't possibly know what thoughts are running through my head. A session of looking at porn is so private and individual and personal and constellates a lifetime of sexual imagery and experiences and curiosities that no one but me knows. People who love to shop or go for walks or unwind by watching television don't need a destination to justify an expedition. Likewise, I jack into pornography for the pleasure of dipping into a world of wall-to-wall dirty pictures.

The first time I remember seeing any kind of porn, I must have been 10 years old, living at Tachikawa Air Force Base in Japan, playing kickball with some other kids. As would happen every so often, the ball got kicked over the wall of a cement square protecting the electrical power generator that fueled the neighborhood. We called it "the hot box." There were DANGER signs posted all over it, and it always felt like you were taking your life in your hands to climb over the wall to retrieve the ball. You could definitely get in trouble if you were caught doing so. All kinds of rubbish collected inside the hot box, and one day I picked up a few pages torn from a Japanese magazine published on really crappy newsprint with a couple of badly reproduced black-and-white pictures of two naked people — not models or pretty people but a completely ordinary goofy-looking man with glasses and a dumpy-looking woman, their naked skin blending in with the white walls of the room and the bed, their bushy black pubic hair drawing the most attention. I doubt if it turned me on, but nakedness was always titillating.

During the same years, I was obsessed with pop music, everything about it. I listened to the radio (the few hours a week when pop music was played on the Far East Network). I watched bands play their hits on the Ed Sullivan Show (all TV shows were overdubbed in Japanese except live performances). I followed the

Billboard Hot 100 charts by way of the printed lists available weekly at the BX, the department store-like "base exchange" whose record section was my home away from home, and I read every pop-music magazine I could get my hands on. Magazines represented the world outside my family and my life as a military dependent. I was most obsessed with *Song Hits* and *Hit Parader* because they printed the words to the songs I heard on the radio. (Some songs I'd never heard so I got to make up what they sounded like.)

The magazine rack at the BX became a kind of temple for me. The rest of the world mattered less than this wall of magazines. The handful of pop magazines drew most of my attention, and I idly flipped through the movie magazines that rested nearby. But inevitably my curiosity zeroed in on *Playboy*, the one magazine in all creation known to include pictures of naked people. It was so clearly an adult magazine, and I imagined that everyone in the store was watching me at the magazine rack, just waiting to pounce on me and scold me if I looked at a *Playboy*. So I would maneuver to hide a *Playboy* inside a movie magazine, in order to indulge a few furtive moments of flipping through the pages looking for naked people. The naked people were, of course, women with acres of smooth white and tan flesh with big boobs, but every so often there would be a hint of male nudity, usually in the regular feature "Sex in the Cinema," which would include racy stills from movies that were rated C for Condemned on the lists posted on the community bulletin board at the church where my mother, my sisters, and I attended Mass every Sunday. I think I can safely say that the first adult man I saw naked was Anthony Newley, who apparently romped starkers in a silly '60s movie called *Can Heironymus Merkin Ever Forget Mercy Humppe and Find True Happiness?* The closest thing to an erotic icon in my youth was the image of John Phillip Law as Jane Fonda's blind bare-chested guardian angel in *Barbarella*.

Standing at the magazine rack looking at these pages, my heart would pound and my blood would race, more with fear of being caught than with erotic excitement. In the barber shop, the Japanese ladies never objected when I "accidentally" brought a skin magazine to the chair to read while they cut my hair instead of *Time* or *Life*. "*Playboy dai jobe!*" they would say. ("*Playboy okay!*") They seemed to enjoy the opportunity to check out the naked girls in the magazine over the men's shoulders. On occasional trips to Tokyo, I would keep an eagle-eye out for newsstands. One particular magazine rack carried two or three smaller-than-average-sized magazines with names like *Physique Pictorial* and pictures of nearly naked musclemen on the cover. But I assumed they were aimed at bodybuilders and professional wrestlers and passed them by in favor of anything with the Beatles on the cover.

Undergoing puberty had nothing to do with pornography or dirty pictures for me. There wasn't any to be had on the Air Force base in Utah where I started making the bedsheets crusty with my adolescent mattress-humping. I fantasized about playing with other boys and seeing them naked. But the only opportunities — showering after gym class or during Boy Scout campouts — were overpowered by crippling self-consciousness and generational modesty. When we moved to Colorado, our former neighbors from across the street in Utah came to visit, and I spent one night and one afternoon frotting my friend Mike fully dressed, which felt great but also dangerous. Everything about sex had to be hidden. Nothing was spoken out loud.

For the longest time, my sex education was conducted through books. My first encounter with gay life came while crouching in the aisles of the Aurora Public Library scouring Jean Genet's *Our Lady of the Flowers*, trying to hide the boner in my shorts from reading about drag queens in prison sniffing each other's farts. The paperback section in one department store had a single copy of *The Sexually Adequate Male* that contained a few paragraphs on homosexuality in a chapter on deviance. The only dirty pictures I remember encountering in Colorado were a pile of black-and-white snapshots that I came across snooping through drawers while babysitting for the family who lived across the courtyard. Pictures of the schlubby husband with a boner, pictures of the schlubby wife naked and laughing, pictures of the two of them together — who took those pictures? They blew my mind. After that, babysitting was all about snooping for dirty pictures, mostly in vain. Occasionally I would find a stash of *Playboy* magazines in a closet. Once, in San Antonio, I showed up for a regular babysitting gig at a neighbor's house just as the young military dad walked naked out of the bathroom, toweling himself off after showering. I beat off to that two-second glimpse for years.

My high school years were an erotic wasteland. I had ardent friendships with girls and crushes on male classmates, along with a childhood sweetheart named Roxanne whom I met in Japan and wrote letters to several times a week for years. But I was a homely kid with a bad haircut and government-issue eyeglasses. No one had the slightest inclination to introduce me to the pleasures of sex. I would have loved for some priest or schoolteacher or gym coach or scoutmaster to take me under his wing, bring me to his house, "show me his etchings," and fiddle with me. When we moved to New Jersey, another big handsome new kid in town named J.R. confided to me that GIs from the base would pick him up and give him blowjobs in their cars. I heard rumors about the football stars at my tiny high school fooling around with each other. No such luck for me.

I didn't start having sex until my sophomore year in college in Houston, which included a semester of one-way sex orally servicing my ostensibly straight roommate, who was 6'6" and hung proportionately. Twice I attempted intercourse with female friends, one pass traumatically unsuccessful, the other brief, pleasureless, and accomplished only by fantasizing about my roommate. And I had a short-lived initiatory affair with the Greek Orthodox priest who was the musical director of our campus production of *Zorba!* There were also a handful of tearoom trysts in the basement of the campus library, very exciting but by far the most outré and unspeakable of my early erotic encounters. Still, in the early 1970s, nothing resembling pornography was readily available. My first exposure to hardcore cinema was watching *Deep Throat* in a special screening at the Rice University Media Center, a weird evening whose context was part sociological, part film-scholarly, solemn and titillating at the same time.

Then I moved to Boston, which was a whole other story. I plunged into drama school, where I met a quantity of openly gay guys for the first time, two of whom I had fleeting affairs with. By New Year's, I had met my first long-term boyfriend, John, who was 13 years older, a recovering alcoholic finishing law school who became a true erotic mentor to me. He schooled me in the matter-of-fact sexual ethos of 1970s post-Stonewall gay liberation. Cruising for sex in public parks, picking up people in bars, having orgiastic sex at the baths, and going to see dirty movies were all acceptable aspects of gay life. John walked me through each of those experiences, either accompanying me in person or giving me detailed instructions so that I could find my way without feeling too embarrassed, intimidated, ignorant, or flummoxed to participate. We didn't have three-ways but we read *Open Marriage* (Nena and George O'Neill's best-seller which was for the 1970s sexual revolution what Dossie Easton and Janet Hardy's *The Ethical Slut* is for the age of polyamory) aloud to each other on a cross-country car trip and had liaisons with other guys separately. He shared with me the collective wisdom that had been similarly imparted to him by his mentors and friends — one of the great advantages for me of being attracted to older men.

In Boston, of course there were porno movie houses, which advertised on the same pages of the *Gay Community News* as the theater reviews I'd begun to publish. But how did I get there the first time? Possibly from going to porn theaters in Times Square when I made theatergoing expeditions from Boston while I was in college. I distinctly remember seeing a movie called *Click Click* in an unusually crowded theater upstairs from a storefront on Eighth Avenue and getting a hand job from a fat bald guy sitting next to me who literally used the classic move of draping his raincoat over our laps to jerk me off. So exciting, so forbidden, so adult and anarchic. Something crucial happened that day — it peeled away a layer of social pretense to reveal the possibility that sex could happen anywhere. As I write about this, I make the connection that a key plot point in the play *Equus*, which I saw when it was in previews on Broadway, was the boy's running into his father at a porn theater and realizing that all the men he saw around him, including his father, had dicks that they sought to pleasure through sex or masturbation. Somehow the notion of older men sitting next to younger men in movie theaters and fondling them under folded raincoats and the notion that men had sex in toilets ("Show hard for blowjob") entered my brain very early on in my sexual career.

This was the time in American culture — the mid-1970s — when pornography emerged from the underground. Porn magazines were no longer hidden under the counter or behind brown-paper wrappers. Innocent *Playboy* spawned more hard-core skin magazines like *Penthouse* and *Hustler* and *Screw* that incrementally expanded the realm of permissible imagery from boob-centered photos of models with airbrushed crotches to full frontal nudity, pubic hair, and penetration, which meant the debut on the scene of penises openly displayed in their engorged glory. And then, for the first time, the emergence of gay porn — not just the closety physique magazines with athletic guys in posing straps and ridiculous props or *After Dark* with its tasteful nude photos of Broadway chorus boys. Now there were *Playgirl*, *Mandate*, *Honcho*, and *Inches* with their smutty stories and multi-page full-color spreads of masculine hunks with mustaches and dangly dicks.

These magazines were as important to me as any assigned reading for my classes at Boston University. I bought them, read them, beat off to them, and collected them. To me they constituted an essential part of a gay cultural self-education. Somehow I always perceived the models in these porn magazines to be idealized male beauties — often too smooth, oiled, polished, shaved, and muscled for my taste. I certainly never considered it my challenge in life to look like them or date guys who looked like them. Perhaps, as Michael Bronski has written, I wanted to be them — that is, to act on my own sexuality as openly and shamelessly as they did.

I gained important perspective on pornography by frequenting dirty movie houses — the South Station Cinema in Boston, most notably, but also the porno palaces in midtown Manhattan (the David, the 55th Street Playhouse, the Big Top, and especially the Adonis). For one thing, the men in the audience didn't look anything like the guys in the movies. The skin-flick patrons were regular Joes, schlubby, scrawny, dressed like businessmen or bums, and yet they gravitated toward the dirty movie house for more or less the same reasons, to breathe the dank air of a temple to male-on-male lust, to watch guys getting it on not only in the movies but in the seats, in the bathrooms, in the hallway or curtained alcove or behind the screen or wherever the spectators huddled for groping and fondling and stroking and sucking each other. (See French filmmaker Jacques Nolot's *Porn Theater* for a remarkably honest depiction of the very particular behavior that goes on in such an establishment.)

Porn movie theaters were never as raunchy or transgressive as the sex clubs that emerged in the 1970s, whose denizens were the true outlaws and edge-seekers of the gay sexual subculture. They certainly weren't like the bathhouses that were designed to facilitate the full spectrum of sexual activity between consenting adults, with private cubicles, steam rooms, showers, lockers, and towels provided. Porno houses catered to a different clientele, more anonymous, not necessarily committed to a gay identity, relatively inexpensive to patronize and therefore available to students and unemployed and marginal folks, and they were open during somewhat normal business hours rather than the middle of the night. Samuel Delany's 1996 essay "Times Square Blue" provides an intricately detailed personal/sociological documentary tour of that now bygone scene.

For me going to the dirty movies was never just about watching the movies. For one thing, they were mostly quite slow-moving and boring. But also I'm more of a tactile guy than a visual guy, less of a voyeur than an active participant. Dirty movie houses brought out the bold, the exhibitionistic, the compulsive in me — if sex was possible, sex was mandatory. The sex was virtually never transcendent. It was often quick, grubby, incomplete, smelly, a little sordid. Yet somehow the contrast between the sex on the screen and the sex in the seats was thrilling and exciting to me. It felt like the ultimate rebellion, an eruption of male sexual lust and abandon not contained into private spaces but spilling out into the movie theater. Another paradox of porn: it is a form of entertainment culture where the standards are very low. When you're horny or lonely or young or deprived, anything will suffice to feed your hunger.

16
PORN AS LIFE FORCE

Andy Warhol said that when he was in high school he wanted a friend, but then he got a television and he didn't need a friend anymore. Pornography is like that.
— Andrew Holleran, "Notes on Porn"

When Enrique's brother-in-law had a heart attack, he dropped everything and flew to San Antonio to be with his family. His brother-in-law declined steadily. After two weeks in the ICU, they brought him home, where he died. Enrique was stressed out the whole time so he sat in the dining room of his sister's house every night looking at porn on Tumblr late at night. He wasn't jerking off, he said, but connecting to archetypal cock worship. "Each regular guy on a Tumblr blog is inhabiting the archetype of those Greek gods in the pantheon," he said. "I don't go to church anymore. I do my worshipping on my computers and mobile phone."

After his brother-in-law died, when he got back to Miami, Enrique spent three days in a funk, getting high every night and jerking off to porn. Finally, on Sunday, he decided he would take a break from that. Around 10 pm, he answered an ad on Craigslist and ended up at 11:30 fucking a gorgeous 23-year-old — "an Adonis!" — on the pool table in his family's cement-floor garage.

> *Porn films invade our lives in a way "legitimate" movies do not; rarely do we want to watch "real" movies every day, in the morning and evening, or know that when we go home we can watch more; but with porn we can and do. Having porn on your laptop is like having someone waiting for you when you get home. Pathetic, but true.*
>
> *— Holleran*

I experienced the healing power of porn most strongly in the 1980s during the darkest days of the AIDS epidemic in New York City. As a friend and as a volunteer for Gay Men's Health Crisis, I would visit young guys — guys my age — in hospital rooms and rub their swollen feet, hold their hands while they dozed in a medicated haze, and do my best to engage in chipper conversations about movies and plays and anything but their skeletal frames and the KS lesions covering their arms and their faces. Afterwards, I would often stand in the stairwell or stop on a street corner and cry for a minute at the sad, savage spectacle I'd just left. Then I'd head straight to the Adonis to spend an hour or two watching guys fuck on the screen and fool around in the seats. Was I numbing my grief? Maybe. I thought of it as visiting a temple to gay male desire, an affirmation of life.

> *[XTube] is an endless stream of porn films, constantly replenished, so that the scene you watch on Page 1 before you go to bed may be on Page 10 when you get up the next morning if you go looking for it, as you may*

The Paradox of Porn

well do. Xtube.com is like a river of film that is flowing even as you sleep, a vast conveyor belt moving images forward, so that you really must make a mental note of where the film was when you first saw it if you want to find it again.

— Holleran

I never used to be someone who got mesmerized by porn. I know people who can disappear into X-Tube and not come up for air until hours have gone by. I considered myself capable of superior restraint.... until my husband turned me on to Maxtor's Hard Drive. For some reason, this Tumblr blog got me hooked. The pictures and videos Maxtor (whoever that is) posts are pretty damned hot, but there's hot stuff all over the internet. I think what's fiendishly addictive about this is that each page has a finite number of pictures – and pardon me while I escape over there for a minute, strictly for research purposes – yes, roughly 15 pix per page. He adds to it all the time, but you can keep clicking backwards into the archive. And then it becomes like potato chips – just one more, well, okay, three more, three at a time, or just til the teakettle screams, or just til 11:30, okay, 11:45...you see where I'm going with this.

And then there's Snowball-Southgermany....

The more you watch porn, the more you may wonder: Why go to the grocery store? Why write your novel? Why not just stay home and watch Bareback Threesomes on pornmd.com?

— Holleran

Mack took a high-powered job at a medical center in Virginia that is a good career move and maximizes his skills as an administrator. But it keeps him perpetually on the verge of burnout. He uses porn as an efficient way to keep in touch with the life force that pulses underneath his workaday world. He shared his unedited porn-diary with me.

"I'm exhausted from a month of 14-hour days (commute+work) at my new job and this week in particular. I need to go to bed at 9 pm to get the 9 hours of sleep that makes me healthy and in a good mood, but I hardly ever do. In theory I could sleep in tomorrow since it's the weekend but I'm used to getting up at 6:00 am. I plan to watch about 15 min. of 'Lotto and Pablo' from Tylersroom tonight, just to remind myself that there is life somewhere. The characters are a little smooth and not too terribly interesting to me, sort of vanilla, but I think one of them is pretty, creamy skin, bland but pleasant features, actually his torso looks amazingly long to me (mine is fairly short). It should remind me of life before I drop off to sleep. I'm sure I'll touch my genitals while watching but I'm not horny at all. ... Ten minutes later I'm totally hard, turned on by the pretty one lying with his chest across his friend's lap, pants down and lovely but full of sexual delight. ...Then I got hooked and horny, so fun to watch the vulnerable bottom's bottom, his anus, the pretty guy's dick in it, the pretty guy's humping motions. Love watching the bottom's genitals get smaller and larger. Cum on his balls looks like icing on cakes. That was a 37-minute video, and then I watched 5 minutes of another with a white guy with a big thick dick, also a cool face. But it's bedtime. I'm motivated to hook up with one of the tops or top couples on a4a tomorrow."

* * *

It is a pleasure to do these things – to drink tea, to drink wine, to read, to listen to music, to exchange flirty messages with sexy guys, to organize quick-n-dirty blowjobs with strangers – and I deeply believe in pleasure. That life is made for pleasure. Epicurus was right to claim that pleasure is the highest good. And yet I want to be attentive to the sneaky ways that habit turns pleasure into indulgence and then compulsion and addiction, into experiences that numb my brain and my heart, numb the pain of facing deeper dilemmas not so easy to identify or resolve or tolerate. What is it that overindulging these pleasures means to anesthetize? The ticking clock, the knowledge that life is short? What's the line from Lanford Wilson's *The Mound Builders?* "To blind myself to the passing moon."

17. PORN AS COMIC ENTERTAINMENT

Paradox: Porn is dead serious. No laughing in sex space.

Porn is hilarious. From ancient Greece to contemporary Bhutan, erect penises are intrinsically comical.

Pornography needs no intellectual justification, any more than comedy does. Comedy either makes you laugh, or it doesn't. Porn either turns you on, or it doesn't. And porn is often quite funny. Half the pictures I save to my camera roll or on my Tumblr blog make me laugh AND turn me on.

Yesterday I watched a 12-minute video of a stocky fellow in a green t-shirt energetically blowing someone through a glory hole he'd installed in his living room (a gay interior design element that never made it to *Architectural Digest*). At about the 10-minute mark, a cat jumps up onto the kitty condo in the background and prowls around, glancing at the action and at the camera indifferently. Along the same lines,

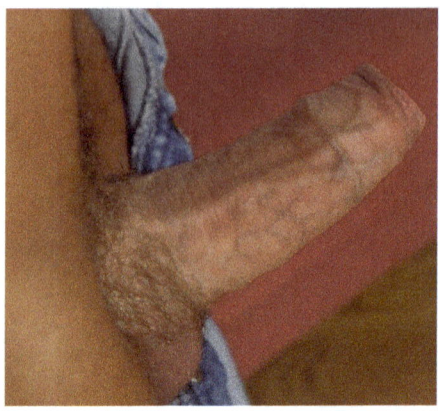

the website LuridDigs.com mercilessly reviews the interiors visible in amateur porn and profile pictures, providing hours of fun.

Long before homemade smartphone porn, Boyd McDonald made a name for himself publishing accounts of real-life sexual encounters that were more arousing than most porn stories but with a droll humor and an appreciation for the comic aspect of smut. His pioneering zine, *STH (Straight to Hell)*, subtitled "The Manhattan Review of Unnatural Acts," introduced reader-written accounts of Kinsey-worthy sexual escapades with headlines like "The Heartbreak of Butt Pimples" and "I Slept With My Nose Up His Ass." He edited several volumes of "true homosexual experiences" from *STH (Sex, Meat, Smut, Flesh, Juice, Cream, Wads)* and inspired countless gay zines, most notably *BUTT* magazine. McDonald was gay porn's Hunter S. Thompson. His commentary distinguished itself with its knowing juxtaposition of journalistic observation and raunchy colloquialism.

Less intentional forms of porn as comic entertainment show up in catalogue descriptions of porn videos that beg to be recited aloud — in a British accent, perhaps, or channeling Howard Cosell:

> MORNING WOOD: Synopsis
> *The sun isn't the only thing rising. Arms wrapped around each other, hands roaming, eyes opening with a smile...TitanMen exclusives **Dario Beck**, **Jesse Jackman** and **Nick Prescott** each have a partner that makes Morning Wood relief an instant away. With their hairy muscle bods lying next to each other, **Jesse Jackman** and **Josh West** wake up in each other's arms—Josh's massive meat soon buried inside the bottom's holes. A kiss on the couch heats up as **Dario Beck** and **Tom Wolfe** exchange sucks, Tom then taking charge of the dark-haired hottie in a romantic fuck. The bed boners of **Nick Prescott** and **Tyler Edwards** quickly disappear in each other's mouth, Nick staying stiff as he gets fucked by the beefy top.*

Ditto the captions on Tumblr blogs:

> *Training a faggot to understand he is property, and he exists to be used and give pleasure to his Superiors. Hard and relentless throat fucking is a very effective training tool - it requires absolute focus from the faggot in order for him to deliver the worship he knows he must give. All other thoughts are driven from the faggot's brain as he must think only of keeping up with the throat fucking. The only thought that can remain is the ecstasy of total and absolute submission.*

Even just URLs on XTube are horrifying and funny at the same time. See, for instance: http://www.youporngay.com/watch/7753856/if-you-crave-for-a-brutal-fuck-in-your-tight-ass-or-deepthroat-enjoy-this-gay-kinky-group-sex/.

Or maybe the comedy is more intentional than I'm giving them credit for. John Preston, author of *Mr.*

Benson, which *Penthouse* called one of the ten best S/M novels ever written, said he thought it was a comedy. "I remember laughing out loud as I typed up the adventures of Jamie, the perfect slave, as he tried to fulfill the desires of Mr. Benson, the perfect master."

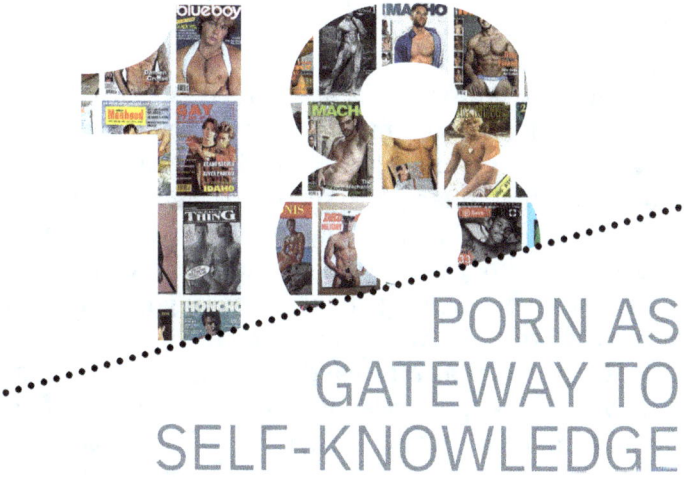

PORN AS GATEWAY TO SELF-KNOWLEDGE

John Preston gave a lecture at Harvard University called "My Life as a Pornographer" in which he made some important historical observations about the place of pornography in gay male culture. "I think that explicit erotic material...in the late 1970s and the early 1980s, was especially important to gay men because we were all in open rebellion over the way our sexuality had been repressed. We were breaking out in our lives, and people were looking for a literature to reflect that breakout." Preston became friendly with Anne Rice, who besides writing best-selling novels (*Interview With the Vampire*) published pornographic novels under the pseudonym A. N. Roquelaure. Rice once remarked that pornography wasn't a place where one lived but a place where one visited. "It was a statement that made me want to envision what that vacation would look like," Preston said. "What would sex be like when it didn't have to be fueled by alcohol or drugs or repression or any of the rest of it? What would totally permissive, totally consensual sex look like?" His question comments sadly on the reality that many gay men require drugs and alcohol to stave off the shame and inhibition instilled from years of repressing their sexuality.

Onetime editor of *The Advocate*, the first national gay newsmagazine in America, Preston made his name as a writer contributing fiction to the gay hardcore magazines that emerged in the 1970s such as *Mandate* and *Drummer*. "Those magazines contained stories and articles about the gay life that was coming into the open; they were writing about it, making it more real to those who hadn't yet experienced it."

Here's a real-life case in point: My client Bobby's first experience of sex was jerking off in the basement with his best friend Jeffrey looking at his sister's *Playgirl* magazine. They did that several times, never kissing or touching each other. Jeffrey told Bobby about a gas station where he could buy gay magazines. This became its own totally thrilling adventure, complete with the huge fear of getting caught. Bobby plotted each expedition meticulously: what other merchandise he would buy as a decoy (a candy bar or Hostess Twinkies), the nonchalance with which at the last possible moment he would add to the purchase what he really came in for, being careful to pick just the right three-pack of discount-priced outdated magazines, how long he would be in the store altogether ("very in-and-out, like *The Thomas Crown Affair*"). Then he'd jerk off at night in bed or into the toilet or shower (he had his own bathroom). He jerked off a lot, two or three or four times a day every day from age 13. He learned to masturbate from a book his mother gave him. Pictures of naked men were always thrilling. His first fantasies were of seduction – being seduced, disrobed, touched...then he'd shoot almost immediately. There was a huge fear of exposure around all this.

After the gas station, he discovered there was a gay bookstore in Atlanta called Christopher's Kind. He called the store and asked if he would be arrested if he bought a magazine (being underage). When he finally got up the nerve to go, it was like The Promised Land for him. But his fantasy of being arrested seemed almost like a request, a way to ask for help or intervention, wanting to unburden himself to his parents.

In college he had what he calls "an Evelyn Waugh-like relationship" with another guy that ended badly. He halfheartedly dated women until he was 30. He still had a rich autoerotic sex life with porn magazines, though one suffused with guilt and shame. Periodically, he would swear off the stuff and dispose of his stash, which would inevitably get replaced. He once went to a porn theater in San Francisco, again fantasizing that some catastrophe would happen (his car would be towed) and people would find out he was gay that way. Finally, he came out to his parents after a cocktail party where family friends made strenuous efforts to set him up with girls. His parents were supportive without wanting any details.

He moved to Philadelphia for business school, and the internet came along. From 1996-99 he used Gay.com to connect with men. He met five people, other closeted guys finding their way. Their explorations were tentative, confined to making out, stroking and sucking, with a major fixation on cleanliness. Anal sex remained strictly taboo. He never had sex with anyone more than twice. They would show up at 9:30 and leave by 10:15.

For Bobby, there was a big split between his embodied sexuality and his sexual fantasies of ferocious male energy. He is in a sustained emotionally secure relationship now, but their sex life lacks the aggression he craves. Bobby always initiates and on the rare occasion that anal sex happens (once a year), he is the top, although he longs to be penetrated, longs to be the object of another man's fierce lust. Pornography serves an important purpose of feeding his soul by keeping the furnace of his erotic imagination well-stoked, even if he can't bring himself to integrate his fantasies into his sexual behavior. You could say that his interaction with pornography is where his uninhibited erotic self reaches its fullest existence.

19
EVOLUTION OF HOOKUP CULTURE

I'm writing this at a house in the Catskills loaned to me by a gay married couple who've been together for 20 years. They met in Washington, D.C., through a personal ad in a gay newspaper, before the days of computers, chat rooms, online dating sites, and hooking up via social media apps. Meeting through personal ads involved a lot of steps, a lot of time, and a lot of patience. In order to receive replies, you had to rent a post office box. Then you had to compose your ad, describing yourself and what you were looking for both vividly and succinctly, counting the characters to make sure they fit in the three-line format of personal ads. You mailed in your ad, or took it in to the newspaper's office, and then you waited a week for it to appear in print. Then you waited for replies to show up in your post office box. If you wanted to respond to an ad, you needed to send a picture of yourself, which meant bringing a negative to the nearest Fotomat, dropping it off and then coming back to pick up the copies you made. Then you had to write a letter, address an envelope, put a stamp on it, and drop it in the mailbox. And then you waited to see if the guy you wrote to would get in touch. If you were lucky, he would write back or give you his phone number, and then you'd plan to talk and then meet in person. The whole process could take weeks. The anticipation could be both agonizing and romantic, an old-fashioned courtship. But if the match didn't take, then you'd have to start all over again.

Flash forward 20 years. Today the vast majority of us are online, with access to e-mail. Most people have smartphones with cameras and internet access. Taking and sending pictures is easy-breezy. You can create a profile on a social media app (Grindr, Scruff, Manhunt, Mister, GROWLr, Adam4Adam, etc.) in a few minutes and start meeting people the same day. The waiting time shrinks exponentially. Anticipation gets foreshortened. Expediency trumps romance. Hijinks ensue.

Alex is a businessman who frequently travels to South America for his work. He finds himself buying Armani shirts and schlepping them to Buenos Aires for a total stranger he's been chatting with on Grindr. The Armani guy was cute, but he spoke no English and didn't kiss. Alex sucked him off and there was some sweet close contact. Afterwards Alex emailed him to say "Let's get together again." The guy wrote back asking for an Abercrombie & Fitch sweatshirt and said, oh by the way, I'm married. Another game-player named Joey wrote him 40 texts adding up to a whole lovemaking scenario that turned Alex on wildly, even though Joey has otherwise resisted any attempts to actually get together. Instead, Alex hooked up with Sebastian, who spoke really good English, wasn't especially attractive, and had bad breath so wasn't kissable. He walked into the hotel room and immediately got on his knees to blow Alex, then hopped on the bed on all fours wanting to get fucked. Alex felt momentarily empowered to do so, but then the guy wanted to suck his dick some more. Alex said, "Whoa, mixed messages!" The guy said, "Yeah, I just broke up with my boyfriend." Alex ended up saying, "You know what? Just leave."

When he got home to his apartment in Chicago, Alex was so horny from not having gotten off that he hooked up with a guy who wanted his dick sucked. Five minutes into it Alex realized that wasn't really what he wanted. He was angry, tired, sad, and frustrated.

Here's the shadow side of Gay Hookup Culture in a nutshell – guys wanting to connect, sexualizing all emotions, expecting everybody to Perform Like Porn Stars, and nobody getting what they really want. Or worse, they wind up feeling more damaged, more lonely, more caught in a no-win situation.

SQUIRTING

JOCK SHOTS is a nut-busting collection of the most juicy, ball-draining cum shots from your favorite bound jocks! Load after load after dick-squirting load, witness the endless amounts of bound jocks' explosions for your repeated pleasure. Featuring the climactic eruptions from Dylan Roberts, Sebastian Keys, Derrick Hanson, Josh West, Samuel Colt, Casey Williams, Will Swagger, Drake Wild, Troy Collins, Brandon Jones, Ryan Lynch, Shay Michaels, Brian Davilla, Kevin Case, Spencer Fox , Tommy Deluca, Alex Summers, James Jamesson, Sebastian Keys, and Lucas Knight! Watch now while your hands are still free!

Paradox: a) the standard "money shot" in porn exemplifies the AIDS prevention motto "cum ON me, not IN me," thereby providing a healthy and exciting education in safer sex. b) guys love watching other guys spurt in porn and then demand that partners produce for them, thereby creating an unhealthy pressure to perform.

Dennis e-mails me: "I've been dating someone I met on Match.com. It's pleasurable but non-committal. I find myself working too hard, wanting to please him. We have protracted kissing and unhurried foreplay. He wants to please me, and I want to please him. I have problems achieving orgasm. I feel like I've let him down if I don't produce a nice load. We end up climaxing by stroking ourselves. I can hold a hard-on and enjoy it, until it gets to be time to perform that final coda. When I look at porn, I search out extremely explicit refined images having to do with beards and architecture. I'm trying to push myself into the mold of Dennis who cums on cue."

Illustration by Josman

A perfect example of the paradoxical impact of pornography on real-life sex is how men ejaculate. The evolutionary function of ejaculation is to inseminate, so it is originally meant to happen internally. Embracing the pleasure and joy of masturbating means overcoming the ancient Biblical prohibition against "spilling one's seed." But in pornography, ejaculation is "the money shot." It is the be-all and end-all. It is the punctuation for virtually every scene you'll ever see in pornography (gay or straight). It is, let's face it, right up there with cute pet tricks as the most thrilling act to capture on film. Women have the awesome power of giving birth. But men have this super-power of making a slick white juice explode out of their penises — it flies, it shoots, it spurts (and sometimes it dribbles and it drools). It usually feels really good, and it's almost always exciting to witness.

Before pornography became a de facto instruction manual, the main reason men would not ejaculate inside their partners was contraception. Since that isn't an issue between gay men, sex with ejaculation meant cumming in someone's mouth or up his ass, a pleasurable act of communion (cum-union). In the evolution of pornography, still photography focused on beautiful bodies and erect penises, not spunk so much. A puddle of jizz isn't especially exciting in a picture. But when it comes to porn films and videos, ejaculation is the visible proof that climax has taken place, reinforcing the idea that sex is all about getting off. Sex is not complete without ejaculation. Sex is not sex without it. So the guy who's fucking pulls out and shoots all over his partner's chest or ass or back or genitals. The guy who's getting blown pulls out when he's close and squirts on his partner's face or chest. As a depiction of sex it's kind of weird — it portrays what might previously have been called "coitus interruptus" as the point of the story.

Some guys have always liked jacking off together. It's one of those adolescent mythological rituals, the circle jerk, checking out other guys' equipment, competing to see who can shoot the farthest. (More of a fantasy for most boys than a reality.) Before AIDS came along, it was a minority preference, a kind of fetish, a way of experiencing your masculinity in another guy's presence that didn't involve insertion (the receptive role being seen as passive, therefore feminine, therefore threatening to the masculinity project). But certainly after the emergence of AIDS in the early 1980s, any "exchange of body fluids" — or even the appearance of sweat, spit, or ejaculate — became scary, dangerous, potentially lethal. Suddenly, pornography's fixation on the money shot inadvertently morphed into responsible modelling of safer sex. Jerking off together shifted from tame, Boy Scout sex to a preferred activity.

"On me, not in me" was a key mantra in sex-positive AIDS awareness campaigns, though even mutual masturbation could seem perilous after AIDS. Frightened gay guys could get very creative imagining possible ways of transmitting AIDS — what if cum lands on my hand and I've bitten my fingernail? What if it gets in my eye? What if I have some imperceptible cut on my skin? Better to jerk off alone. For lots of gay men, both adults who were already sexually active and teenagers just coming into their sexuality, sex in the 1980s and '90s meant jerking off alone, with porn as a safe and pleasurable companion.

It's undeniable that watching a hard cock ejaculate is very exciting. The male body responds to pleasure by ejecting semen out the tip of your cock! A homemade spectacle a man can produce for his own entertainment! It is a little miracle of orga(ni)smic hydraulics. Much about ejaculation is unpredictable and uncontrollable. You never know how much juice is going to spurt out, how far it's going to fly, how many spurts a single ejaculation will produce. In a certain way, they all look alike, especially if you look at a lot of them. You can literally spend all day long viewing cum shots online. It's so banal watching guy after guy spurt spurt spurt

spurt spurt, and yet no amount of Hollywood car-chase scenes interest me as much as watching a guy jerk off. It's like seeing rainbows, fireworks, waterfalls, lightning flashes — natural processes that almost always draw our fascinated attention. I suppose it's like watching sports. If you're not an aficionado, baseball or golf or tennis all looks the same and gets boring pretty quickly. But if you're a connoisseur, you enjoy every tiny variation. Every ejaculation is individual, unique, and therefore riveting.

The fetishization of cum has become its own realm of pornography. Blowjob scenes used to build to a climax involving the guy pulling his dick out of the sucker's mouth and letting the camera capture the sight of jizz flying through the air. Even the porn tradition of the facial observes the safe-sex rule of "on me, not in me." But these days edgy porn makes it a point to show the cock spurting into someone's open mouth, the receiver holding it on his tongue, not necessarily swallowing it but sloshing it around his mouth, drooling it back out and down his chin. The transgressive realm of bareback porn generates its audience by showing men (sometimes tattooed with biohazard symbols indicating that they're poz and proud) fucking without condoms, the epitome of bad behavior in the days before PREP for those who have any exposure to HIV education and awareness. We love to watch it on screen and experience it vicariously because we're not going to do it in our real lives. Or it gives us permission to do the forbidden thing we're longing to do.

For gay men, cumming inside someone's ass is rarely carefree. It's the most intimate form of sexual communion, often reserved for committed partners. With casual partners, taking cum up your ass can be seen as the ultimate irresponsible activity, since it's the primary way of contracting HIV. Risk-taking always has its erotic appeal to some guys, though, and just like "barebacking," "breeding" has become another contemporary meme, a perfect example of fetishizing cum. It remains to be seen how the approval of Truvada as "pre-exposure prophylaxis" for HIV (PREP) will affect the appeal of bareback porn. With the increased incidence of condomless fucking among gay men under the guise of "treatment as prevention," will bareback porn seem less edgy?

Curiously, even in bareback porn, it's rare that a top actually cums inside a bottom, although that is the most transgressive/exciting act — but if you can't really see the proof, how do you know? So now a whole new set of porn protocols exist: 1) the top fucks bareback until he gets close, pulls out and shoots on the guy's asshole, then fucks the cum back inside him. 2) the bottom squeezes the load out of his ass, literally making the cum the star of the show taking a curtain call. Sometimes (Treasure Island Media videos make a specialty of this) an ardent cum-hound is standing by to lick the cum dripping out of the just-fucked asshole or collect it into a cup which the bottom or some other available pervert drinks up, smacking his lips with relish.

Before ubiquitous porn video, guys engaged in mutual masturbation for the simple pleasure of jacking off together. Now there's an additional layer of pleasure that comes from witnessing in person something you've seen online hundreds of times. Real sex has become live pornography — real in Jean Baudrillard's postmodern definition of reality as "that which can be reproduced." Maybe you're being conscientious about "exchanging body fluids." Maybe you just don't like the taste of cum or aren't prepared for fucking. And maybe it's just that there are times when it's fun to Perform

Like a Porn Star for your partner — to put on a show consciously, consensually, voluntarily.

Personally, I'm not much of a masturbator. I'd rather have sex with another person than with myself. And if I'm going to squirt, I'd rather do so while merging physically with my partner. One of the benefits of being in a committed relationship is having the option to negotiate unprotected sex and to experience the exquisite intimacy of sharing semen without fear. I'm not immune to the pleasure of watching other guys ejaculate. But since I've given erotic massages professionally for more than two decades, I've had hundreds, if not thousands of opportunities to witness cocks spurting with joy. My husband, on the other hand, has not, though he has a robust relationship with pornography and jerking off has been his primary sexual activity for most of his life. So for him it is a special treat when I cum "on him, not in him." To witness the entire build-up of orgasm in real time, to hear the sounds your partner makes, to feel the shaking and the surges of energy from a few inches away is like sitting in the front row of a concert by a favorite singer you've watched on video a million times but never seen live.

Problems arise when guys pressure their partners to ejaculate when they don't want to. "OK, I came, now it's your turn." "Cum for me, baby." "If you don't cum, I'll feel badly." "If I can't get you off, I'm a bad sex partner." "If you don't cum for me, it means you don't love me, or you don't find me attractive." There is a presumption, based on what we see in porn, that ejaculating is always easy and always pleasurable. The reality is somewhat different. Some guys cum really fast, which makes them extremely self-conscious and protective about ejaculating too soon because then the energy drops and the encounter is over abruptly.

You might be surprised to learn how many guys have difficulty cumming — because of medication they're taking, because of party drugs they're on, because (paradoxically) they're so accustomed to jerking off to porn alone that it's difficult if not impossible to ejaculate in someone else's presence.

Aging has an impact on ejaculations as well as erections — it can take much longer to cum and the refractory period (how long it takes to build up a head of steam again) gets longer. Guys who have been treated for prostate cancer usually stop producing ejaculate. Guys with bigger, thicker dicks often take longer to shoot. Even guys who have none of those conditions can get anxious when sex becomes about performance rather than pleasure and connection. Biochemical research tells us that anxiety releases chemicals into the bloodstream that directly block or counteract arousal. Insisting that your partner Perform Like a Porn Star and squirt when he doesn't want to is a form of coercion that is less playful than, say, climax denial. It's not satisfying, not fun, and in fact can verge on being cruel.

I'm thinking of Gerald, an overweight Filipino man in his sixties who's had a raft of health issues, including surgeries on both his hips and both his knees. He's been treated for prostate cancer, depression, and a heart condition. He walks with a cane, and before he retired from his civil service job in city government he often had to use a wheelchair to get around. Nevertheless, he watches a lot of gay porn and perceives it as a representation of the sex most gay men have. He himself never had a youthful period of sowing his wild oats. He's in a long, caring but sexless relationship with a very proper, buttoned-down Englishman. Gerald has a large penis and he has difficulty ejaculating under the best of circumstances.

It usually happens when he's masturbating but even then there's no guarantee.

When he turned 60, he became determined to do whatever it takes to Perform Like a Porn Star at least once before he dies. Since he had never penetrated anyone, he wasn't sure he could sustain an erection in order to do so. He'd tried Viagra and Cialis but they didn't produce erections reliably enough for his taste. So when he learned that porn stars inject themselves with Caverject, he asked a urologist to prescribe it for him; when his doctor refused, he went online and found a source for it on the black market. Then he searched for sex workers willing to experiment with him. He found several and cultivated relationships with them. He was overjoyed to find that he could manage penetration, but he could not make it all the way to ejaculation while fucking. He somehow marshaled the stamina to "pound" his favorite escort for 15-20 minutes, which was thrilling for the recipient but exhausting for Gerald. Once the escort ejaculated, then he demanded Gerald ejaculate as well, in order for him to feel like he'd done his job. Gerald would sometimes pretend to ejaculate or claim that he'd experienced a retrograde ejaculation (in which the semen travels backward into the bladder). Gerald felt so unhappy at the prospect of disappointing the sex worker that he considered filling a syringe with lube, fucking the guy face-down, and then shooting the lube on his back and pretending it was cum. Never mind that Gerald was the customer, whose satisfaction you would think takes priority. For him, his own pleasure and satisfaction took a backseat to the purely conceptual goal of living up to the standards of male sexual performance set by porn.

Some guys don't need partners to exert pressure on them to ejaculate — they supply the pressure internally. Neil, a handsome magazine editor in his late thirties, came into therapy because of intense anxiety over his inability to cum in the presence of a partner. No one had ever complained about this, but during sex there would almost always come a time when Neil would become highly self-conscious imagining that his partner was getting bored, thinking it was time for him to squirt. The more pressure he felt, the higher his anxiety became, and the less likely he was to achieve orgasm. Again, pleasure was left in the dust. A masturbation enthusiast, Neil never had trouble ejaculating on his own — whether it took five minutes or 45 minutes didn't matter because there was no one else there to prove anything to. His anxiety had gotten to the point where he was reluctant to date anyone because the prospect of performing sexually had become so fraught with expectations he was afraid he could never meet.

Stewart, an office manager for an internet provider, had the opposite experience — he could ejaculate quickly, often quicker than he really wanted to — with the same consequence of starting to dread dating for fear of disappointing his partner by cumming too fast. He was chronically walking a tightrope, trying to steer guys away from his erect penis, and either the anxiety would cause him to lose his erection or his partner would be so eager to please him that he would squirt fast. Then Stewart would lose interest in continuing the intimacy and feel guilty about not reciprocating.

Needless to say, these scenarios never show up in porn videos. The question of whether the sex is satisfying doesn't factor into porn. It's all about the money shot, about Getting the Job Done. And that matches many men's experience of ejaculation. A lot of guys jerk off every night at bedtime to put themselves to sleep. Other guys jerk off two or three times a day, or more, as a way of managing stress. If that works for you, who am I to argue? But as a pleasure activist, I always want to champion keeping pleasure in the picture. When getting off becomes a quick and habitual process, it sometimes loses any flavor whatsoever.

How do you get the pleasure back? It certainly doesn't hurt to scale back the frequency of ejaculation. I'm told that in Chinese medicine there is a guideline for men — take your age, double it, and divide by ten. That's the number of days that ideally should elapse between ejaculations. I've shared that formula with plenty of men who do the calculation in their heads and go, "Whaaaat? Ten, eleven, twelve days???" It's not a rule, but you can try it yourself and see what impact that has on your orgasm. The principle is that when you discharge semen, you discharge energy (*ching chi*). If you ejaculate more often, then it's helpful/healthy to make extra efforts to replenish your *chi* through diet, exercise, and meditation. I've certainly found that spacing out my ejaculations makes each one much more exciting, powerful, and pleasurable.

That doesn't mean not masturbating for a week at a time. It just means cultivating an awareness of the distinction between self-pleasuring and getting off, and between orgasm and ejaculation. I received a life-changing education in tantra and Taoism through Joseph Kramer and the Body Electric School, whose protocol of Taoist erotic massage gave me an important new paradigm for experiencing my sexuality in addition to Getting It Up and Getting It Off. By raising and circulating erotic energy around the body through breath and touch without the goal of ejaculating, it's possible to reach heightened states of erotic arousal and enjoy the experience longer. Instead of feeling pleasurably depleted after ejaculating, choosing not to squirt creates the possibility of feeling extra-alive, extra-alert, spiritually blissful, creatively recharged.

Whether in a massage context or while self-pleasuring, one way to punctuate the experience — to create a climax without ejaculating — is to do what's called "The Big Draw." After building energy through the combination of breathing and cock-stroking, you take a big breath and hold it as long as you can while squeezing all the muscles in your body, mentally picturing the energy traveling up from the base of your spine to the top of your head. When you finally exhale, a rush of energy travels through your body that can be extremely pleasurable. With practice, it's possible to have a rip-roaring full-body orgasm, complete with involuntary spasms of energy that can go on for a few seconds or a couple of minutes, without ejaculating.

This pleasure is almost entirely internal. There's often nothing much to see, which is why you don't see Taoist eroticism portrayed in porn. It's something you have to experience for yourself. Ditto the variety of practices that come from the practice of tantra. The word tantra gets thrown around a lot, to the point where it can mean vastly different things to different people. Tantra refers to an ancient practice of meditation that involves envisioning lovers intertwined as a metaphor for merging with the divine. In eastern philosophy and religion, tantra is regarded as a deep, often quite abstract practice. The Dalai Lama, for instance, teaches Buddhist devotees a variety of tantric meditations that involve elaborate visual patterns, a way of focusing the mind's attention that is purely internal. In the West, tantra has come to be associated with sex — indeed, specifically with the rock star Sting, who let it be known that his tantric practice allows him to have sex with his wife for hours at a time without ejaculating.

Anything sex-related that shows up in the media almost immediately becomes a subject for mockery and sniggering. But the practices involved with tantric sex definitely lead to an expansion of how you experience your sexuality and so have tremendous value for people who have found intercourse-to-ejaculation to have limited or diminishing appeal. Taking your time, building heart connection slowly through touch and breathing, exploring the dance of male and female energies, hanging out with eye-gazing in stillness, creating ritual space with music and candles — these are some delicious ways of creating intimacy and pleasure that you're not likely ever to see in porn films because they're not photographable, they're slow-moving internal experiences of communal exploration and satisfaction. And it takes tremendous courage and intention to seek out instruction and willing partners. Exploring tantra and other forms of non-ejaculatory lovemaking also requires recognizing the imprint of porn and actively choosing to set it aside as the template for sexual interaction.

Pleasure can look a lot of different ways, not all of them photographable. Whether you squirt or decide to contain your ejaculate, what happens immediately after the climax is a special and important part of sex, an opportunity for sinking deep into physical surrender and spiritual communion with yourself and/or your partner that you'll never see represented in pornography. It's an opportunity plenty of people skip over out of habit, training, or lack of exposure to alternatives. As Andrew Ramer says in *Two Flutes Playing: A Spiritual Journeybook for Gay Men*, "If you ask most men about the three levels of post-orgasmic states, they would probably tell you they are cleaning up, pissing and falling asleep. Or sleeping, waking and doing it again. Or cleaning up, getting dressed and getting out of there." In an essay called "Places to Go When You Come," Ramer discusses how to use orgasm as a doorway into altered states of consciousness. He points out that orgasm is a microcosm of the Big Bang: "Whenever anyone has an orgasm, for a moment they tap into that same energy and…re-experience the beginning of the world." He offers his own version of the three levels of the post-orgasmic state: swimming in the realm of pure eternal bliss, floating back to the time before you were born, and then remembering all the moments that led from your conception up to the present moment. And he encourages men to gradually develop the ability to stretch out the moment after orgasm to stay in and explore each of these three post-orgasmic states for longer and longer periods of time (or no-time) rather than jump right back into your skin.

Gunther Nitschke, a German architect who has studied a wide variety of meditation techniques in Japan and India, wrote a whole book called *The Silent Orgasm* about the spiritual benefits of prolonging the orgasmic experience. While respecting Taoist, Tantric, and yogic teachings about controlling the breath and the retention of semen, he asserts that it is only during orgasm that the individual achieves a state of authentic well-being in which time and space lose significance. He advocates sex as meditation: "physical hyperactivity, hyperventilation or deep catharsis…in order to trigger utmost relaxation, silence and stillness, a state of choiceless awareness and non-judgmental acceptance." Similar to Ramer, Nitschke sees orgasm as a doorway into transpersonal consciousness, the merging with the universe from which life came and into which it disappears. A loftier vision of what happens after orgasm than you're used to? Don't knock it 'til you've tried it.

There will always be guys whose sexual imagery is steeped in the dominant narrative of pornography, for whom rough sex is exciting and masculine and fulfilling. Stewart told me he broke up with his first boyfriend because of their incompatibility — the boyfriend wanted porn sex, and Stewart wanted the kind of connected lovemaking that his boyfriend dismissed as "lesbian sex" (a curious, not uncommon expression reflecting the tenacity of old, unexamined gender-role stereotypes). I'd like to think that it's advantageous for good lovers to cultivate a varied repertoire. If someone doesn't want to cum fast or has difficulty cumming at all, it seems cruel to force the issue. It seems more pleasurable and satisfying to develop ways of communicating what's desirable in an encounter and to find a way to make it acceptable not to squirt without feeling like someone has failed to do his duty. As with the issue of maintaining erections, my mantra is "Measure the pleasure."

21

FUCKING

Probably the biggest gap between porn-as-entertainment and porn-as-education falls in the area of buttfucking. It is the central act in more than half the porn clips you can find online, and for the most part what you see in porn bears very little resemblance to how people organize anal sex for pleasure and connection in real life.

In a typical porn scene, guys proceed from preliminary making out, stroking, and sucking to anal play without words. Magically, it's clear who's the top and who's prepared to bottom. If there's been any preparation to get fucked on the bottom's part (i.e., cleaning out), we don't see it. Rarely do we see someone applying lube. If there is a condom, it's unusual for us to see it being removed from the packet and rolled onto the guy's dick. A lot of times it's hard to tell if that shiny surface sliding in and out of someone's hole has a condom on it or if it's just lubricated.

In porn, the adjustment time from approaching

penetration to full penetration is a matter of a few seconds. Foreplay consists of the top licking his hand or spitting in his palm and wiping it on his dick before shoving it in. The guys who are fucking may change positions from time to time, but there's no way of knowing what motivates the change — has the position become uncomfortable? Are they bored? Does the cameraman want to shoot the action from a different angle?

Once penetration has been achieved, the action can get pretty boring pretty fast. In, out. In, out. In, out. In, out. So in porn fucking tends to escalate to pounding, along with punching and spitting, since aggression looks like action on screen and keeps our attention. It's rare and usually riveting to see eye contact or kissing between guys who are fucking. To maintain viewers' interest, a third party will show up, or a group scene occurs. Extreme variations such as spit-roasting, tag-teaming, and double-penetration have become widespread, almost obligatory. These scenarios have become so prevalent that they've become normalized, commonplace, standard repertoire for the modern gay man.

A lot of fucking in porn doesn't look very pleasurable to either participant. The action is staged in a way that is advantageous to the camera trying to zoom in on the action but that requires the players to adopt contorted positions that don't look natural, comfortable, or fun. Often the bottom looks like he's enduring something awkward if not painful. Sometimes what we're watching looks very close to rape. Meanwhile, the top is thrusting, thrusting, pounding, pounding, sweating, grinding, hoping and praying to stay hard and to get himself aroused enough to shoot, which means pulling out (if there's a condom, we rarely see it come off or disposed of) and squirting on his partner's face, chest, torso, cock, balls, butthole. Maybe the bottom gets off. Maybe he doesn't. What happens next? Cut! Whatever happens after fucking — cleaning up, cuddling, complaining, first aid, laughing, instant replay? — remains a mystery.

And that's the good stuff, the full-length fuck scenes from commercial studios. On Xtube and Tumblr blogs, you can narrow your search and your viewing to watch hours' worth of variations on any tiny increment of the encounter: the dick reveal, insertion, the money shot, squeezing the load out, etc. This is the basic formula of pornography as entertainment, whose goal is to get you aroused and get you off, with efficiency if not expediency. It's a form as codified and formulaic as any other genre of entertainment (the murder mystery, Kabuki theater, the police procedural, the Broadway musical, the opera) or spectator sport (tennis, golf, baseball, football). The format is so strong and predictable that the fun of watching has everything to do with witnessing the minute variations.

The problem arises when you attempt to use what you watch in porn to inform your intimate encounters at home. You can start off trying to reproduce your favorite porn scene while fucking with someone, but pretty quickly you come to gaps where pertinent information has not been conveyed. Again, it becomes like trying to put together furniture from IKEA from those wordless instruction handouts that come in the box. Some people can manage it. For others, it takes all day and it never turns out looking right.

* * *

Here are some events that show up in porn films all the time that, in my estimation, are way less fun to experience in reality than they look in porn:

1. having someone cum on your face (aka, getting a facial) — it's pretty hard to avoid getting it

in your eyes, which stings. Not fatal, but an immediate buzzkill.
2. double penetration — usually accomplished by having the bottom sit on one cock and the other fucker sliding his dick in on top of the other's. This takes a lot of maneuvering and is hard to maintain for very long and mostly turns out to be a kind of erotic acrobatic stunt that's more fun to check off the "Done That" list than actually physically pleasurable to any of the participants.
3. being penetrated at both ends, on your hands and knees, one cock in your mouth, one cock in your ass (aka, getting spit-roasted) — it looks very hot but again turns out to be an acrobatic challenge for the bottom to keep his head up and do a reasonable job of not mangling the dick in his mouth while the guy fucking him is thrusting his hips energetically. It may be intermittently pleasurable for the bottom to be filled up at both ends but the thrill is primarily a mental one. The fantasies and piggy self-reflections of the bottom may make it absolutely worthwhile, but it's often less exciting than it looks.
4. Lucky Pierre aka daisy-chain — the guy in the middle is fucking the guy in front of him and getting fucked by the guy behind him. Again, the idea can be very exciting, and the visual can be hot, but it's a rare individual whose erotic body is sufficiently multi-centered that he can stay sufficiently hard to penetrate while being penetrated.
5. being fisted — although it shows up in online porn venues as if it's a standard item on the menu, taking a fist up your ass or sliding your

hand into someone's ass is way less common than sucking, fucking, and stroking. It takes a considerable amount of preparation and aptitude to be a fisting bottom, and it takes a significant amount of care, attention, patience, and responsibility to be a fisting top. I've lost count of the number of guys I've met who've watched videos online of bottoms with gaping wide-open asses and who wish they could train themselves to open up like that. The most common errors include going too fast and concentrating on a goal rather than enjoying the journey, which depends almost entirely on trust and communication with your fister.

Anyone who thinks they need to be prepared to participate in such activities to be a sexually functioning gay man has my permission to think otherwise.

* * *

In my experience and observation, a satisfying sexual connection has three essential components:

- **P** — paying attention to your own Pleasure
- **C** — Connection to your partner, emotionally/spiritually/energetically
- **M** — Mechanics (what goes in and out, what goes up and down)

When couples have problems with sex, nine times out of ten it's because these three elements are out of balance. Usually there's too much emphasis on the mechanics. Performance anxiety creeps in. Sex starts to feel excessively acrobatic. What started out as fun has turned into work. The best thing to do then is pause, take a breath, ask yourself "Is this feeling good?" and then do whatever it takes to re-route your activity, suspend what isn't feeling good, and return to simple pleasure.

That may mean making an effort to set aside whatever images from porn you're consciously or unconsciously trying to emulate. What does real fucking look and feel like when there aren't cameras around? Slow insertion, checking in with your partner to see if you're going too fast or if there's pain (there shouldn't be – don't override it). Apply plenty of lube at the beginning and be aware that you may need to add more as you go along. Instead of steady pumping, you can stop and start, hold still with your cock deep inside. Check your dick as you pull out, wiping it off before going back in or switching roles.

Beyond the local sensations of insertion and thrusting, there's usually some key activity that makes fucking truly pleasurable. It can be physical or emotional. It could be making out with your partner. It could be cuddling. It could be stroking yourself. It could be changing positions. It could be stopping and having a conversation. It could be switching from attention on you to attention on him, or vice versa. It's could be letting go of trying to get yourself off or get your partner off. It's hard to connect to your partner if you're out of touch with your own pleasure. Likewise, when you're feeling pleasure, you're much more likely to feel connected to your partner, and when those two elements are in the place, the mechanics take care of themselves.

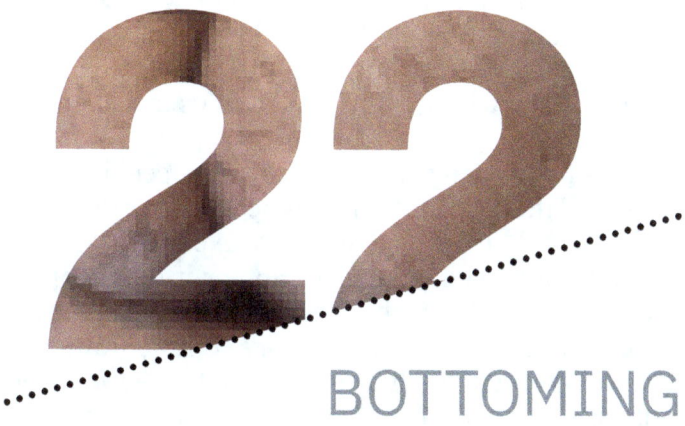

22
BOTTOMING

Bottoming is theoretically one of the prime joys of gay men's sex lives. And it's true that for some people it's absolutely the center of their erotic universe. For them, anal sex is the epitome of "going all the way," the top prize when it comes to intimate companionship. In reality, though, anyone honestly investigating the relationship between men and their buttholes will quickly discover that, in Facebook parlance, "it's complicated."

In my practice as a sex therapist, I counsel many men whose ability to participate in the pleasures of bottoming is compromised by several flavors of fear and shame. I think it's important right off the bat to acknowledge that there are plenty of myths and fears about butt-sex, and it's normal to feel them. People who are new to anal pleasure typically face 1) fear of pain, 2) fear of disease, and/or 3) squeamishness about shit. These are understandable fears to have, and they can be addressed with practical information and communication. Having a sensitive partner or teacher can make a big difference.

But let's face it – you can equip yourself with all the information in the world about safer sex, douching, lube, breathing, and pillow talk... and still be phobic about bottoming. That tells us that shame is in the picture.

There are two varieties of shame I see a lot. We might call the first one "competence shame": Gay porn makes it look like all gay guys are experts at fucking and getting fucked, and if I'm not, or if I don't enjoy it or I don't want it, that means there's something wrong with me. Then there's what's commonly known as "bottom shame": If I like to get fucked or even fantasize about it, that means I'm less than a man. Bottoming brings up deeply held, often unexamined attitudes about gender roles, power, desire, being gay, being yourself. What stops men from embracing the pleasure of bottoming almost always has to do with the meaning we attach to the experience.

Where do those meanings come from? And is it possible to shift those meanings?

First of all, even to talk about bottoming requires running the gauntlet of casually brutal colloquial speech, where "getting screwed" or "getting fucked in the ass" means to be exploited, humiliated, or otherwise degraded. That language stems from the stereotypical straight male's horror of being penetrated, which gets exclusively associated with being gay. "Virtually all men in our society learn negative attitudes toward homosexuality early in life," wrote Jack Morin, a San Francisco-based psychologist, in his valuable book *Anal Pleasure and Health*. "Those who turn out to be gay internalize the same anti-gay messages, sometimes to a greater degree than straight men." As Morin points out, men's fear of homosexuality conjures the more basic fear of being viewed by oneself and others as unmanly and feminine. "A great many men try to suppress, at all cost, the soft, receptive aspects of themselves. They fear their masculinity will be compromised and, therefore, their value as people reduced."

"For men, weakness and vulnerability and need are negative qualities associated with women," says Michael Cohen, a gay psychotherapist in New York City who has taught classes on anal pleasure for the Body Electric School. "Being submissive for someone else's pleasure may feel like being passive, like our long-suffering mothers, whom we both love and despise. And sometimes just the desire for love, for attention, to be opened up can feel humiliating and helpless, the opposite of strong and self-sufficient."

Gay guys who've been tormented in childhood for being sissies learn that it's bad enough to be considered effeminate. If you believe that the only real man is the stud who gets hard and does the fucking, then getting fucked threatens to make the fear you're not a man come true. "There's a surrender of what we think masculinity ought to be when we take a man's dick into us," says Keith Hennessy, award-winning performer and sex educator in San Francisco. "That's why so much porn shifts that moment to rape, to being taken, to not being responsible, to not choosing. The top knows that the bottom can't willingly give in to his desires, so the top forces the bottom for his own good."

The internalized homophobia that Morin described shows up in the way gay guys, even among ourselves, adopt a smirky attitude toward bottoming. To call someone "a big ole bottom" is usually a put-down in the form of a comic punchline. The drag queen working the crowd picks out an audience member and asks, "Are you a top or a bottom?" And before her target has gotten two words out, she howls, "Bottom!" The essence of the joke is: Don't kid yourself, honey, nobody thinks you're a man, you're just a Big Girl. (That kind of joking strikes me as surprisingly hostile, as when straight guys use "cocksucker" as an insult. Shouldn't a word that means "pleasure-giver" be the highest praise?)

Working with sex therapy clients, I often notice that all roads lead to the same conclusions: "There's something wrong with me…I'm not man enough…I'm weak, I'm no good, I'm foolish." That tells me that we're not just dealing with sex; we're really talking about shame. Who I am is bad and wrong. At the core of bottom shame is the very human struggle for self-acceptance, and it can be a lifelong task to work through it.

In his book *The Velvet Rage*, Alan Downs suggests that gay men have their own specific journey when it comes to working through shame. "It was early abuse suffered at the hands of our peers, coupled with the fear of rejection by our parents, that engrained in us one very strident lesson: There was something about us that was disgusting, aberrant, and essentially unlovable," Downs writes. "To experience such shame, particularly during our childhood and adolescent years, prevents us from developing a strong sense of self." That sense of self develops from a strong identity that is validated by your environment. However, a gay man afraid to show himself for fear of rejection may create a "best little boy in the world" persona just to please others. Paradoxically, the validation earned by that persona ultimately doesn't feel very satisfying, Downs notes, "since authentic validation can only occur in the context of one's true, authentic self."

The good news is that it is possible, with patience and support, to work through shame and early conditioning to arrive at a place of authentic self-validation. (*The Velvet Rage* closes with a smart list of "Lessons on Being an Authentic Gay Man, Or What Mom Didn't Know and Dad Couldn't Accept.") Virtually every gay man who enjoys the pleasure of bottoming has encountered the same cultural prohibitions and potholes of shame as everybody else but has assigned a different meaning to sex, power, and pleasure, usually by focusing on his own body rather than someone else's opinion.

"There's power in rejecting rules and expectations of what others think a man should be," says Hennessy. "The hungry or willing bottom definitely has power. Getting fucked is generally very active. You want it. You ask for it. You let it happen. Often you prepare (cleaning outside and/or inside) and even rehearse (with fingers or dildos)."

Pornography isn't always effective as sex education – it can be intimidating and misleading – but you don't have to look far to discover men getting fucked without sacrificing their masculine identity. In fact, some consider getting fucked to be the hallmark of "taking it like a man." Scott Smith, webmaster of BillinExile.com, has written extensively about serving in the US Marine Corps, notoriously if surprisingly tolerant of rampant man-on-man sex. "With Marines I always found a willingness to play either role with a high degree of comfort and definitely without shame," Smith told me. "In the Marines, sex is what men do together. It doesn't matter if you're top or bottom, you're still having an extremely manly experience."

To view sexual role-playing as a multiple-choice question rather than an either-or proposition is another way that men learn to enjoy bottoming. In other words, welcoming your feminine side as well as your masculine side, the giver and the receiver. Clinging to masculinity and fleeing from femininity leaves you cut off from half your humanity. There's wisdom in finding a balance.

My favorite example of how that plays out in the arena of buttfucking comes from Tom Spanbauer's novel *The Man Who Fell in Love With the Moon*. The hero of the novel, Dellwood Baker, tells his young protégé a fable about a mythological character he calls the Wild Moon Man.

"Story goes he takes you to the bottom of the lake to his home, and teaches you how to breathe water instead of air. If you don't trust him and do what he says – you drown and they find you floating the next morning. But if you do trust him and do as he says, story goes, when you start breathing water, that muddy old hairy goat turns into a beautiful, strong warrior and he teaches you many secrets about the true power of being a man.

"When the Wild Moon Man takes you underwater, to the hairy rusty mud, he's taking you to your asshole. To the place that's as female as a man can get. You find your natural male power through your asshole, not your dick. You find your prostate. Fire down there under all that mud and hair and water. You find in yourself what most men love women for: their ecstasy, their hole into the other world. By receiving a man into you, by receiving a man like a woman, by being as female as a man can get, what you find — if you don't drown — is the beautiful warrior in yourself who knows both sides."

"Men like us are lucky," Dellwood says, "We've learned to breathe water."

* * *

The flip side of bottom shame is bottom envy, which has exploded exponentially in the age of internet porn.

Peter is an intelligent, hard-working professional in the television industry whose social anxiety and perfectionism feed on each other. He feels naïve, inexperienced, and not proficient at sex at all. He was fucked a couple of times 20 years ago and enjoyed it. Throughout his thirties he had medical issues and his libido was low. Now that it's back and he's watched a lot of porn, he wants to enjoy buttsex the way guys in videos do. But in real life it's painful and awkward. "Watching guys getting fucked in porn makes me want that. They make it look flawless, fun, and smooth. In real life, it feels clumsy to me. It feels like playing Twister on a rocky ship. And I have a huge cleanliness issue — I worry about being dirty." Given his strong aversion, I wondered if anal sex simply falls in the category of things that play better in fantasy for him than in real life. But porn has so forcefully implanted the notion that a "normal" gay sex life includes fucking that Peter can't view its lack as a matter of choice, only as deficiency. "Saying to myself 'I just don't like getting fucked' feels like a cop out, taking the easy way out, that I'm too lazy to do the work."

A similar mythological belief exerts pressure on Tom and Jerry, who have been a couple for more than 20 years. They both enjoy fucking, neither enjoys getting fucked, so the fucking part of their sex lives happens with other partners, and they'd like to share more pleasure between themselves. Jerry feels like a failure because he can't take Tom's huge thick cock. Tom has a lot of psychological baggage, including religiously induced sex shame, cultural prohibitions (Latino machismo) against being the receptive partner in anal sex, and a heavy attachment to looking at porn (he watches a lot of it and jerks off to it four or five times a week). Tom admitted that he tends to get very frenzied when turned on and just wants to fuck until he shoots. He was a bit spoiled by his first boyfriend, whom he could roll over and fuck in the middle of the night. For them, fucking was easy, whereas Jerry's first experiences with fucking were fraught with fear of pain and anxiety about disease.

On top of all that, they are socially prominent as a gay couple. They assume that all successful gay couples fuck and that they are in some way "letting down the team" because they haven't figured out how to enjoy buttsex together. The assumption is that guys who just blow each other are less gay or committed or intimate than guys who fuck. At the heart of the matter is that each of them feels sadness and frustration that he can have very intimate, ecstatic fucking experiences with other guys and not with the man he really loves. Although it takes some selective interpretation to get there, porn has given them the impression that in the sexual circus acrobats must also be jugglers, and sword-swallowers must also be trapeze artists. For Tom and Jerry, it's not permissible to have a specialty act.

* * *

And then there is what I suppose could be called "bottom indifference." You might be surprised to know there is quite a vast population of gay men for whom the question "Top or bottom?" is completely moot because they're just not into anal sex. My friend Wayne falls in that category.

"Coming out with gay porn, it seemed like a given that I'd love assplay. I *had* to — I was gay," he told me. "I've actually never found it the least bit interesting or erotic. I'm just not wired that way. And yes, watching porn made me think I was a horribly deficient gay man. I tried getting fucked. Nothing. Not physical pain, not emotional distress, not AIDS panic, just nothing. I tried fucking other guys. Same thing. While porn showed me that there were other things I could do, it also showed me that these things *inevitably* led to fucking. When I first met my husband Mark in 1989, fucking didn't come up for a while. Then one day, he said he wanted to fuck me. I started to cry. If fucking was really an important part of sex to him, then this relationship was never going to work out. Even though I could do it once in a while, I never actually *wanted* to do it. Mark and I did it a couple times then agreed that we didn't need to keep doing it. Fucking is a very tiny part of his erotic imagination and not a part of mine at all. Now I just tell people that I don't fuck—and, more importantly, tell them what I *do* like doing: I'm a cocksucker. So much simpler."

One of the great personal challenges for any mature adult is to cultivate your own sexual pleasures free of the pressure to conform to someone else's standards of behavior, fantasies, expectations, or preferences. Happily, the payoff for undertaking such a challenge can be measured in self-acceptance and sexual satisfaction. For gay men, that means proliferating abundant options when it comes to buttsex beyond Top and Bottom. Gay sex therapist Joe Kort champions the identity of "Side" for guys who are more inclined to swap oral sex than to fuck. I recently saw someone on social media identify as "Middle" – witty and provocative. The transgender community has developed a rich variety of designations to describe those who reject the gender binary. The same opportunity exists for rejecting the anal-sex binary. Instead of viewing it as instruction manual, let gay porn provide pleasure and arousal for anyone who wants to witness and vicariously experience buttfucking whether or not they ever partake of it themselves.

23
DADDY/BOY LOVE, POWER, AND MASCULINITY

Of all the role-playing scenarios that excite the gay male imagination (master/slave, coach/athlete, cop/civilian, doctor/patient, big brother/little brother), surely none is more potent than daddy/boy. The energy that gets activated between two men when one of them says "Show Daddy your butthole" is so deep, profound, and erotic that we can only call it mythological. The interplay of strong, protective daddy with adoring, obedient boy uniquely combines love, power, and masculinity in a way that Carl Jung, visiting his local leather bar, would call archetypal, meaning that it goes with the territory of being human. It's not that everybody is turned on by daddy/boy fantasies, but we can all locate ourselves along the spectrum of being, having, or wanting a good Daddy.

What does it mean to engage in daddy/boy fantasies? And how does that dynamic play itself out in gay male relationships? For one thing, it's a mistake to assume that all daddy/boy relationships are alike.

For some, daddy/boy is confined to sexual situations, and those can range from playful verbal banter to heavy-duty power-exchange and everything in between. For others, the daddy/boy energy carries over into other emotional and social arenas. While some gay men have memories or fantasies (happy or unhappy) about sex with their biological fathers, most daddy/boy erotic play has nothing whatsoever to do with real-life incestuous desires.

It's not unusual for men to have mixed feelings about their daddy/boy fantasies. Neil, a magazine editor in his mid-thirties, is drawn to sturdy, butch men who radiate competence, confidence, and self-assurance, qualities he would like more of himself. His rational mind is reluctant to name the object of his desire as Daddy, because the thought of sex with his own father is repulsive. And he wants to be seen as an equal partner in relationships, not some kind of "kept boy." Nevertheless, he can't deny that his strongest sexual arousal kicks in when he receives praise for being a "good boy" while pleasuring a partner he's dared to call "Daddy."

"Daddy" and "boy" name states of mind and don't necessarily signify age difference. Likewise, not all intergenerational relationships operate on a daddy/boy basis. Still, there is a big connection between the two. In his 1975 study *The Homosexual Matrix*, psychologist Clarence Tripp offered an astute analysis of relationships, asserting that the emotional side requires rapport (similarity) and the sexual requires contrast (difference). Men and women are sufficiently different to give heterosexual relationships an automatic charge; gay relationships often thrive when sharp variations in age, race, background, or social level create what Tripp calls "the frictions that whip up erotic intensity."

Jake and Joe are a classic example. Jake was a tall, lithe, 23-year-old dancer when he met Joe, a closeted 40-year-old businessman. For the first several years they were together, the contrast gave their connection a red-hot intensity. Joe was Jake's erotic ideal: a big, hairy, ethnic Italian "straight" guy who liked to sit back and get taken care of. And the more codified their talk and touch was, the better. Boy got a lot out of pleasing Daddy, and Daddy got to bestow a blessing by affirming Boy's sexuality.

Perhaps inevitably, things shifted as Jake got older, more successful professionally, and beefier physically while Joe stayed the same. Jake began to chafe at the narrow strictures of their sexplay and longed for more erotic reciprocation than Joe was equipped to provide. Now they face the challenge of discovering a new sexual dynamic that satisfies them both. Interestingly, it's not just Joe who struggles to allow more flexibility into the daddy/boy dynamic. Jake is so used to Joe being Old Reliable that it's hard for him to believe it when Joe asserts his interest in trying something new.

Getting stuck in rigid role-playing is one liability of daddy/boy relationships. It's understandable, if erroneous, to assume that in every team of lovers, Daddy is the designated Top and the boy is the Bottom. In power dynamics, yes. In terms of sexual position, not necessarily. As Gordon – a 42-year-old landscape architect who has been an active leather top for twenty years – memorably put it, "Sometimes Daddy likes to get his kitty punched."

Frank is an experienced player in the BDSM world of power-exchange, and Ernesto, his boyfriend of five years, is an enthusiastic newcomer. Their age difference – Frank is 62, Ernesto 42 – heightens their daddy/boy dynamic. Frank loves to tie up and dominate his boy; Ernesto loves to earn his daddy's love by submitting. This works well when they make use of what they know about creating ritual space where clearly defined intentions and roles amplify both sexual excitement and emotional connection. But when you're living together as a couple, the lines can get blurry. Problems emerge when Frank's pleasure in controlling Ernesto strays outside of sexual settings – demanding that he go to a certain movie or eat a specific food. Then Ernesto feels manipulated and rebellious. Obversely, sometimes Frank feels vulnerable and wants some nurturing that his boy hasn't developed the capacity to offer, and Ernesto feels like a failure.

That's not necessarily a bad thing. The shadow side of the boy's reverence for the masculine ideal can manifest as a tendency to locate that masculine essence as exclusively outside of oneself and letting sexual competence (Sucking Daddy Off) substitute for healthy development in new directions, professionally or emotionally.

As Pat Califia points out in the introduction to the erotic anthology *Doing It for Daddy*, Daddy-boy relationships are a form of mentoring. "Too many young men still have to struggle alone with the question What does it mean to love or want another man? What kind of person does that make me? What will it do to the rest of my life?" And the rewards of mentoring go both ways. The advantage for the designated boy centers on the opportunity to receive the particular masculine love that a tender and nurturing Daddy can offer. For the daddy figure, receiving attention from younger men by modeling the virtues of stability, caring, and perseverance gives new value to the experience of aging.

This trade-off echoes the basic concept of imago

therapy, a widespread form of couples counseling created by Harville Hendrix (author of the classic volume *Getting the Love You Want*), which is that we instinctively choose our partners for a reason. Usually, it has to do with making up for something we didn't get from our parents. But here's the deal: the healing comes not just in, say, getting from your partner what you didn't get from your biological father but also in developing inside yourself whatever qualities you need to achieve your full potential as a human being. And – as daddy/boy enthusiasts know – not just because it's good for you, but because it's hot. The success of porn filmmaker Joe Gage's *Dad* series owes a lot to their ability to dramatize the heat and playfulness of daddy/boy dynamics, which sometimes capitalize on faux-incestuous fantasies and sometimes simply tap into the inherent erotics of difference.

24

THE GIFT OF DESIRE

"Ask for what you want" is advice that's easy to give but often strangely difficult to practice. What gets in the way of identifying our desires and sharing them with others? Growing up gay, we probably learned early on to view our deepest desires as shameful, socially unacceptable, or at the very least subject to other people's negative judgments. No wonder we're a little gun-shy when it comes to letting others know what we want, especially in the realm of love and erotic play.

As a gay sex therapist, I spend a lot of my working hours listening to people talk about the nitty-gritty details of their sex lives. I meet a lot of smart, soulful, intelligent men frustrated at their inability to find love and connection. One of the themes that comes up again and again has to do with asking for what you want.

- Edwin enjoys bottoming in anal sex, yet he needs his partner to go slow, to tune into his body signals, and to use a certain amount of lubrication. All reasonable requests, but he

can't bring himself to mention these things so tends to avoid anal sex altogether or to assume the role of penetrator to please his partner.
- On Mitchell's second date with a guy he really liked, they had good sex, and Mitchell would have liked to stay the night. When his partner didn't extend the invitation, Mitchell dressed, left in a huff, and never saw him again.
- Bill is deeply committed to recovering from his addiction to crystal meth, and now he is reluctant to socialize at all because he fears that if he meets someone in a bar and goes home with him, there might be drugs around and he won't be able to resist using.

For a reasonably intelligent adult with functional communication skills, it would seem to be an easy enough task to say things like, "I would love to get fucked – can we take our time and use plenty of lube?" Or "I would love to spend the night with you – how would you feel about that?" Or "I would love to spend more time with you, and it's important for me not to be around drugs – can we make an agreement about that?" But the actual process of formulating those sentences can be remarkably daunting, nearly impossible. Which tells me that the struggle to ask for what you want is a deeply embedded human phenomenon that deserves attention and respect.

Many gay men live with the nagging feeling that they missed that day in school when everybody else learned to identify their desires, to inhabit them, and to express them to others. Mostly, as gay kids, we were shamed for our erotic desires. We absorbed the message that our hunger for touch and affection, wanting to see and hold other guys' bodies (or, let's be honest, their penises) were bad or wrong and we should keep them hidden away. Sometimes we learned that lesson overtly by being punished, harassed, or bullied for showing our desires. But sometimes we picked them up indirectly from the absence of positive expressions of same-sex desire. Either way, we developed a hyperawareness as a defense mechanism. Any hint of desire can feel like a threat to survival: am I going to be okay, or am I going to get beat up?

If we're lucky, we grow up to find pockets of safety and trust and connection, but that fear of disapproval lingers as an archeological layer. And other fears sneak in on top of that. Shame about sexual desire gets easily wired into shame about any form of non-conformity. Many adult gay men live with a huge amount of anxiety about being ridiculed for their taste in food or clothes or music, being considered a freak or a geek. We live in a culture where we're inundated with reality-TV shows about being people being ruthlessly evaluated, declared to be the weakest link or the biggest loser, having their outfits or their talents or their behavior scrutinized and dished to filth. I notice men in their twenties and thirties especially susceptible to this fear of stating a preference or standing out from the crowd, lest they be judged harshly.

When it comes to sex and intimacy, I'm seeing on top of shame and fear of judgment a crippling kind of perfectionism, a fear of Doing It Wrong. Some of that I trace to the ubiquity of online porn, which can be extremely exciting and entertaining but also tends to depict a limited repertoire of activities performed by a select tribe of super-buff muscly tattooed guys.

Unless you make a concerted effort to explore beyond mainstream commercial gay porn, you get lulled into thinking that's what sex and desire are supposed to look like, and if you can't manage that, or if you don't enjoy that formulaic sort of coupling, there's something wrong with me, and you'd better not even try.

Part of maturing and reaching adulthood is learning to trust your own impulses and your own emotions and your own body. It really helps when you find friends and colleagues and community that support coming out as a positive embrace of who you are. Given that you spend anywhere from a few years to several decades hiding your desires for love and erotic connection, no wonder it takes some time to adjust to letting your partners know what you like and asking for what you want. Here are some things that I have learned that counteract early messages of shame and fear.

1. The late great gay poet Allen Ginsberg once wrote, "Like thought is natural to the mind, desire is natural to the heart." If you're alive, you have desires – it goes with the territory of being human.
2. Your desires belong to you. No one can take them away.
3. A desire is a statement, complete in itself, not a demand.
4. Not all desires are meant to be fulfilled. Whether they're acted on or not, desires contain their own validity and seeds of self-knowledge.
5. The Belgian sex therapist Esther Perel says it succinctly: "Desire requires you to be selfish in the best sense – to hold onto yourself in the presence of another."
6. "Desire is a horse that wants to take you on a journey to spirit." I liked that sentence so much when I heard West African teacher Malidoma Somé say it that I painted it on the wall of my

treatment room and adopted it as a mantra. In other words, whatever it is that stirs at the heart of your desire body connects you not only with pleasure and other people but also with the great mystery of life.
7. A desire can be stated in the form of a fantasy. Again, it can be fun to act out certain fantasies, but it's also true that some experiences play better in fantasy than in reality. And it can be a lot of fun simply to say fantasies aloud.
8. The difference between a desire and a request is that the latter is, at heart, a question – it's a little riskier because it invites a yes or no response. It's good practice to learn to make requests, to be prepared to hear either yes or no, and to acquire the ability to negotiate – which means, if you can, finding a way to turn a no into a yes.

Don't take my word for any of this, though. These ideas only have meaning if you can verify them in your own experience.

Here's an experiment you can conduct to make contact with your desire body and practice giving your gift of desire. Take a piece of paper and make a list of desires. Number one – start with something simple: what I want for dinner. (A salad? A cheeseburger? Herons' eggs whipped with champagne into an amber foam?) Number two – widen the lens considerably: what I want for the world. (An end to hostilities in Syria? No more fracking? Legal marijuana in all 50 states?) Number three – what is my heart's desire. (A boyfriend? An iPad?) Number four – what erotic pleasure I would like to experience today. (A favorite activity? Something new that I'm curious about?) Number five – some desire that doesn't fit into these categories. When you're done making this list, notice what you feel in your body – pay attention to any small sensation and breathe into it. Now pick one of those desires. Stand up and walk around the room saying it aloud 10 or 12 times – softly, loudly, earnestly, in a funny voice, in a foreign accent. Again, tune into your body and notice how it feels internally to speak these desires aloud.

As Alan Downs writes in *The Velvet Rage*, this is how we achieve authenticity, by getting practice at validating our own experience. Rather than waiting for someone else to deliver the stamp of approval for our thoughts, opinions, dreams, and desires, we can give ourselves permission to have them. When you muster the courage and wisdom to share your desires with someone else, it changes what's possible in the room. Pornography can be a valuable tool for identifying and activating desires – that's the role it's best situated to play – as long as you recognize and embrace the freedom to do whatever you want with those desires. Once you can accept your desires as self-knowledge, you have a gift to share with others by letting them know something about you.

And it truly is a gift. Think about it. Surely you've had the experience of hanging out with one or more friends trying to pick a movie or a restaurant. "Where do you want to go?" "I don't know, where do YOU want to go?" Everyone's being so nice, so polite, so afraid of saying the wrong thing, so agreeable, so non-committal – it's maddening. Isn't it almost always a relief when someone steps up to the plate and says, "Let's go HERE"? The same goes for being in bed with someone – trying to read someone's mind to figure out how they're feeling or what's sexually pleasurable can be exhausting and nerve-wracking. You're not doing your partner or yourself any favors by going along with something that doesn't feel good or concealing a desire that you have. If your partner says, "You know what I would like right now….?" aren't you immediately energized and curious to hear?

Malcolm Boyd said it best: "If there is a key to your mystery…let people have it."

25

CONCLUSION

If there's a single genesis for this piece of writing, it might be the non-traditional seder I attended at Randy's house a few years ago. I don't recall whether the canonical four questions were addressed. I only remember the rather startling question that Mathew posed out of the blue: "Why are gay men so bad at having sex?" Since more than half the men in the room had been to bed with Mathew, it took a few minutes to ascertain that he wasn't making an accusation but sharing a genuinely philosophical inquiry. I had plenty to say in response, from my perspective as both an active-duty slut and a gay male sex therapist. And I suppose I've filled these pages with variations on my response that day. Many forces stand in the way of gay men's healthy sexual and emotional development – external shunning and internalized homophobia, religious- and/or family-based shaming, consumer-capitalist encouragement to treat each other and ourselves as commodities – all of which converge in the paradoxical pleasuredome of pornography.

As I've been saying repeatedly, possibly to the point of driving it into the ground, porn has done gay men a great service by providing resonant images that validate our desires, liberating us from ignorance, opening up possibilities, activating our erotic bodies and our imaginations, allowing us to vicariously enact experiences beyond our reach, and giving us a safe way to navigate through times of fear and loneliness. At the same time, porn has done us a great disservice by distorting our ideas of what constitutes normal bodies and normal sexual functioning, liberating some inhibitions but installing others in their place, enslaving us to libidinal impulses at the expense of our health and mental well-being, luring us into dark pockets of obsessive-compulsiveness that leave us isolated and shut down, and modeling a culture of sexual behavior that is so narrow, mechanical, and emotionally bankrupt that we hardly know how to treat each other as human beings.

I could make these observations with the impartial attitude of the anthropologist or social scientist. But I notice that I am not dispassionate about this subject. It pains me to hear and see gay men struggle and fail to find sexual fulfillment. I guess I'm privileged that in my life sex has been a spectacularly rich arena for physical pleasure, self-knowledge, ecstatic embodiment, spiritual wisdom, and intimate relationships. It has been a pathway to deep love and self-acceptance, albeit a pathway lined with plenty of troubling questions, painful losses, and shameful mistakes. And I guess I want that for everyone.

I want, as the poet-sage Smokey Robinson sang, "more love, and more joy, than age or time could ever destroy." I want gay men to drink deeply from the well of horniness that porn both manufactures and feeds. And I want us to be smart and skillful about interrupting the negative consequences porn can have in our lives if we let them go unexamined.

All loving parents try to do everything they can to spare their children pain and sorrow. And all parents in their right minds know that it's impossible and even dangerous to shield children from the full range of human emotion and experience. But as L. R. Knost said, "It's not our job to toughen our children up to face a cruel and heartless world. It's our job to raise children who will make the world a little less cruel and heartless."

So in my guise as community Daddy-Top, I'm going to put on my best battered baseball cap, jockstrap, and lace-up black leather boots to deliver Sgt. Shewey's Seven Take-Aways from The Paradox of Porn, in hopes of inspiring gay men to have better sex.

1. **DON'T CONFUSE THE SEX YOU SEE IN PORN WITH SEX IN REAL LIFE.** At its best, porn is erotic theater for an audience of one. Relish the free play of your imagination without having to cater to anyone else's opinions or preferences. When you're having sex with someone else, be present with that person. Make eye contact. Let yourself breathe. Notice when you're putting pressure on yourself or your partner to Perform Like a Porn Star, and see if you can let that go. Follow what feels good.
2. **CHOOSE WHAT YOU'RE DOING.** Be intentional. There are any number of reasons for looking at porn and/or to have sex. Yes, duh, getting off is one of them, but it's not the only one. You might look at porn and get off to put yourself to sleep at night, to relieve stress and anxiety during the day, or for the sheer pleasure of busting a nut.

You might also look at porn with an intention not to get off, to get your juices flowing for a creative project, to build energy for a playdate, to conduct research about new sexual techniques, or to replenish your catalog of arousing images. If you're someone with a tendency to lose yourself in looking at porn online, consider setting a timer and putting it in another room to see if that helps you enjoy your porn-trance and bring it in for a landing. Same goes for having sex. I can think of a dozen different intentions for having sex, including mutual pleasure, experiencing soul communion, getting high and getting off, getting closer emotionally, exploring intensity, frantically reenacting the last porn movie you saw, trying out fantasies, surrendering to power exchange, laying back and getting done, having permission to touch/suck, doing something different for a change, and resolving conflict. If you're making the same choices over and over again, maybe they're not choices anymore. You may be stuck on an obsession or compulsion. It may be that what you're really craving is something emotional or physical that no amount of getting off will bring you.

3. **DON'T BE AFRAID TO TALK.** One of the pleasures of jerking off to porn is not having to worry about what anybody else in the room is thinking or feeling. But pornography tends to reinforce the common belief that talking about sex (other than moaning "Fuck! Fuck!" or "Verb that noun!") spoils it. I completely disagree. I contend that not talking is a set-up for bad sex. Then you're at the mercy of whatever fantasies are running in each other's brains, which may be miles apart. There's a widespread misconception

that somehow your partner is supposed to magically know what turns you on and if you tell him then he's only doing it to please you. First of all, how's that working for ya? Second of all, don't you want him to please you? How is he going to know what you like unless you tell him? You don't have to keep up a running commentary, and you don't even have to speak in words. I've never met a dog who speaks my language, but every dog-owner knows when the animal is hungry or needs to go out.

4. **EXAMINE YOUR RULE BOOK.** I've noticed that many people conduct themselves sexually according to a list of unwritten, unspoken rules, and they have no idea where these rules came from. For instance, porn encourages sex without preliminaries or pauses. Once you get naked, there's no stopping until everybody cums. That can be exciting, or it can be over, super-quick, or it can become so arduous that pleasure has left the building. That's a good sign that there's a rule here that needs to be challenged. Try something different just for a change. Plus, as the blogger Brian (see Chapter 8) said, it's fun to break the rules.

5. **INCLUDE YOUR WHOLE BODY.** Most of us have a tried-and-true methodology for self-pleasuring — when we do it, where we do it, what supplies we have on hand. We know what works. But the same efficiency can lead to staleness and boredom. Online porn tends to encourage masturbating while staring at a screen, sitting or lying down, in a sedentary or constricted posture, while the rest of your body goes missing in action. Then that same limited amount of embodiment gets carried along to sex with a partner. "Most

Western sex is necrophilia — one dead body having sex with another dead body," as the pioneering sex educator Joseph Kramer once said. Kramer established himself as an erotic visionary by founding the Body Electric School in 1984. During the AIDS crisis, his "Celebrating the Body Erotic" workshops changed thousands of men's lives (including mine) by introducing them to non-ejaculatory sexual practices involving conscious breathwork, massage, and intentional distribution of erotic energy. As the internet took over as our primary source of information and all-purpose porn warehouse, Kramer adapted his teachings to the digital age by creating online courses and videos for his New School of Erotic Touch. He has developed a practice called Porn Yoga. The concept is simple but brilliant: stand up to masturbate. He recommends raising your viewing screen to eye level, free up your hands to touch all over your body, circulate pleasure by thrusting and rotating your hips, imitate the motions you see onscreen, turn your back to the screen sometimes, and experiment with different rhythms, including stopping and starting. Try it. You'll notice the difference right away.

6. **FIND A RECIPE THAT WORKS FOR YOU.** I know there are some recipes for unsatisfying sex, such as saying yes when you feel no and saying no when you feel yes. In my experience, the best way to run a sexual relationship into the ground is to define the terms of sex too narrowly — it's always about squirting, it's always about fucking, or whatever. My own recipe for satisfying sex, as I mentioned in chapter 21, calls for a balance of PCM: your own pleasure, connection with your partner, and mechanics (what goes up and down,

in and out). If you tune into the P and the C, the M usually takes care of itself. Feel free to try that on for size. Revise it, give it a remix, add your own ingredients.

7. **TAKE A BREAK PERIODICALLY.** Whatever pleasures you enjoy almost always benefit from the pause that refreshes. As they say, even the best piece of meat loses its flavor if you chew it too long. That applies to booze, weed, social media, or porn. When you're starting to notice diminishing returns, scale back. Take a week or two off, or a month or two. Grindr and Scruff will still be there when you get back. That includes mobile devices. It's fun to shoot homemade porn. Everybody does it. But just like it can be a drag when you're trying to have sex with someone and he's more interested in his poppers than in you, performing for the camera can become a mindless habit that gets in the way of intimacy and pleasure.

The bottom line is: I want you to do whatever it takes for you to wake up to the joy of life in a body.

APPENDIX: USE OF PORN STUDY (OR, DON'T TAKE MY WORD FOR IT)

In 2014, I conducted a semi-formal, not especially random study asking gay men to keep a diary of their porn-watching for ten days. "Porn" was defined in the broadest possible sense to include not only written stories, commercial videos, and pictures but also social media profiles. Fifty men followed through. The results were fascinating, varied, difficult to quantify or summarize. Nevertheless, having applied some conscious consideration to their porn consumption enhanced the thoughtfulness of the participants' responses to crucial follow-up questions: What are one or two ways that porn has made a positive impact on your life? And what are one or two ways that porn has had a negative effect on your life?

Probably the most significant finding from this study was that the different positive effects outnumbered the negative effects about 2-to-1 — that is, many guys named the same downsides to porn, but what they like and get out of porn is more varied and individual.

Here, in their own words, is how gay men described the negative impact of porn.

1. **Huge Distraction – Waste of Time.** "It's too time-consuming. I'm always edging to get the biggest, longest ropes (but typically worth it)."

   "I will often spend two hours with porn/erotica/surfing when 30 minutes would have been just right."

"Sometime I feel it's a waste of time and a distraction, because I can use porn-watching to avoid other work I need to do."

"Time spent surfing is negative. Could be doing other things."

"I watch it too much. I stay up too late sometimes. It's always on my mind."

"I found myself spending way too much time on apps like Tumblr, so I eventually edited the porn 'pipes' down to one or two."

"Porn is an enormous time-waster, drawing my focus away from my career, routine social opportunities, and mainly my spouse."

"Sometimes I will be late to work or appointments if I need to get off!"

"I'm capable of being addictively swallowed up by it. It can consume a huge amount of time without my either being aware or without my stopping it, even though I am aware how much time is going by."

2. **Implants Unrealistic Expectations.** "It reinforces my dominant visual critical mode, where I can be dissatisfied with my partner or lover because they aren't as hot as the guys in porn."

"Porn has caused me to develop unrealistic expectations for ecstatic erotic experiences."

"It promotes unrealistic beauty standards and sexual fantasies."

"Overexposure to porn, especially idealized body types, has led to disappointment with normal guys and a need to fantasize to achieve orgasm."

"The expectations it raised of what sex would be like and how it worked were less reasonable."

"It certainly sets an unreasonable standard for what we consider an average male body."

"The downside of porn is expecting the same thing in real life."

"It conditions my sexual response and desires so that any potential, realistic sexual partners are never able to live up to these images."

3. **Replaces Real-Life Contact.** "Consuming porn has made it easy for me to avoid real erotic contact."

   "These days porn acts as a substitute for promiscuous erotic contact. That was something I really valued in my life for a number of years, but these days it feels like way more effort than it's worth. I'm not particularly compulsive about watching porn, but I'm aware that it's a kinesthetically pallid substitute for sex."

   "It reduces my motivation to look for dates."

   "It's too easy to get off this way, it keeps me separate and alone, I don't go looking for engagement with others (which can be so much work and so complex)."

   "Sometimes porn makes it too easy to get off. It can be a substitute for the real thing."

   "It keeps me from being as horny for hookups or boyfriend."

4. **Enforces Negative Body Image.** "Sometimes porn leaves me feeling dissatisfied with the way I look, insecure that my dick is too small (always dangerous to make such a comparison with those

who are in porn)."

"It reinforces negative stereotypes and insecurities."

"Porn has led to an unhealthy view of and disappointment in my own size and output."

"Seeing these beautiful men reinforces my already strong negative feelings about my own appearance, 'equipment,' and sexual adequacy."

5. **Steals Energy from Relationships.** "I used to consume pornography. Too much. I would say that it certainly contributed to my most recent break-up. The break-up prompted me to reassess several things about myself, including my relationship with porn. I realized that it was diminishing my sex life rather than enhancing it. We were monogamous but did not consume porn together and so it added up to us having very different sexual experiences and triggers. In a way, I feel that monogamy drove me into the arms of porn. I was not getting the kind of sex I wanted at home and, therefore, felt the need to experience those impulses vicariously. Rather than satisfying me, it served to further drive a wedge between my partner and me sexually. Soon, I was unable to sustain an erection during sex with my partner and that was the unofficial beginning of the end for us."

"I don't always play well with others – need more stimulation to keep it up."

"My porn-watching creates resentment from my partner sometimes."

"It can make me think it's okay to cheat on my boyfriend. We are monogamous."

"Occasionally I've gotten off looking at porn, and then the opportunity to play presents itself, and I'm already spent. It's harder to get hard again as I get older!"

6. **Enables Procrastination.** "Porn sometimes makes it all too easy to hide out or procrastinate or not deal with what is actually more important to me."

   "It did take me away from books and outdoor activities, which I promised myself I would do more of."

   "The main downside of porn is that it interferes with my life as a writer. When I am frustrated by my work, I often turn on the social media sites, despite knowing this could mean hours of lost time. Before the internet, I would step away from the manuscript and read, a process which generally led me back to my work. A site like Manhunt has no such effect."

7. **Numbing.** "Sometimes looking at too much porn leaves me feeling bored — with porn, and with myself."

   "I think it may have desensitized me to value of the human connection."

8. **Portrays a Limited Range of Sexual Possibilities.** "Porn video is always stereotyped and does not have the 'bubbly' effect drawings and photography can have."

9. **Leads to Disconnecting with My Body.** "Porn can take me out of my body and physicality and into my head more than I want it to sometimes."

10. **Creates Addiction/Compulsion.** "I need an ever-increasing flow of stimulus in order to get off,

consuming many images at once. Then I have to take a break to reset my horniness."

11. **Interferes with Healthy Fantasy Life.** "I sometimes feel porn has replaced a healthy fantasy life and become a crutch and an escape when I am feeling depressed. There was a time when I looked forward to being alone once in a while so I could enjoy a good wank. It was fun to explore the internet and various websites. Now I feel I have seen too much of it and novelty is gone. Porn, at this point, has taken away from my sex life as much as it has given."

12. **Perpetuates a Rigid/Narrow Standard of Attractiveness.** "I only find youthful guys attractive, in fact only ones with boyish faces and intense or happy eyes. I am not attracted to guys who look like physically mature adults or are really muscular. Porn hasn't helped with this; I simply avoid looking at characters who look like mature adults. I want someone with whom to escape the world that is run by adults."

"I trained myself to only be attracted to a narrow range of types of men."

13. **Creates a Sense of Inferiority.** "I think the only negative thing I could say it does for me is to almost subconsciously reinforce a belief that everyone else is having great and fulfilling sex lives, even though I know that is not true."

14. **Encourages Isolation.** "Porn has had the impact of making me more self-absorbed, isolating myself from others by only enjoying myself. I miss human contact, that pleasure of feeling flesh against flesh, kissing, etc."

15. **Interferes with Sexual Functioning.** "In terms

of real-life sexual function, I can only get aroused from bareback anal sex, and this may be because it is mainly what I consume in porn."

"The habit of porn-infused solo sex eventually contributed to some issues with performance and self-expectation that took a while to untangle."

16. **Reinforces Negative Stereotypes.** "Being a person of color, I don't like that black men are portrayed as sexually predators. Like the Black Ball series, where a solo white man is gang-raped by a group of aggressive black men."

* * *

And what are the positive consequences of looking at porn?

1. **Affirmation of Desire.** "Porn/erotica, especially the shame-free, gay-lib-influenced stories from the '70s that I first consumed and used in high quantities in the '80s, absolutely helped me claim and reclaim my sexuality and sex-positiveness and feel good about desire and body ecstasy. This was in combination with all kinds of liberation theory — gay, lesbian, anarchist, artist, hippie — that I was also reading and experiencing. But the porn really helped and I think it still does... it helps me connect with gay lives and desires and histories from the privacy of my own bed and imagination."

"It has made me feel at ease with my sexual desires and it has allowed me to accept that my needs and desires are worth taking care of."

"It serves to confirm my interests and desires. Since so many sites are very specific, it helps me to know that many others share the same tastes. It is, in effect, a way for me to keep coming out to myself by recognizing that my feelings are 'normal' – also very important that my feelings are shared by many, many others."

"It makes me realize that sexuality is universal — not something to be hidden and never discussed."

2. **Exposure to a Range of Body Types.** "I have to give a shout out to small-cock blogs and amateur videos on Xtube because many of those images are hot and it helps me to see myself as hot too."

"Porn lets me see that other guys are not always six-pack models."

3. **It Models Shamelessness.** "There is a lot of good amateur porn out there. All kinds of guys are open-minded and piggy enough to enjoy being filmed. Porn provides good images of how me and my contemporaries feel about themselves, instead of self-loathing as they age."

4. **Creative Inspiration Beyond Sex.** "Porn contains old and new expressions of visual interest and seems unlimited formally (drawings, paintings, photography). It's inspiring to me as an artist. It mixes lust, desire, and something free and exciting."

5. **Complements Partner Sex.** "Porn plays its part in sexual satisfaction when no shared sex can be had; it does not compete with the real thing."

"Porn has allowed me to be sexually active in between boyfriends with a minimum of trouble."

"It's a way of maintaining a minimal erotic life while I'm living alone."

"It was really helpful during a period when I really just wanted to stay single to get over a previous relationship. It was a good filler."

"In the absence of a sexual partner, it keeps my sexuality from going dormant or becoming just a memory."

"I have a greater libido than my partner. Porn takes pressure off of him!"

6. **Orgasm Booster**. "It's assisted with so many beautiful orgasms in my life."
7. **Expands Sexual Self-Knowledge.** "Porn has helped me identify what I like, what turns me on, and it's also allowed me to explore fantasies and impulses."

    "Because I tend towards systemic analysis, at a certain point I had seen/read enough porn that I could study patterns about my desire – both what it wanted to be and how it was being constructed by social norms (including gay norms or alternative culture norms). Porn became a way to study my sexual responses and turn-ons (and -offs) and to look at the complex space between inner and outer influences on our sexuality/desire/identity."
8. **Activates Aliveness in the Body.** "At those times when I'm feeling more withdrawn, more cerebral, or perhaps overburdened by petty things, looking at porn can bring me back to my body, to paying attention to what it is like to have a body, to live in a physical world."
9. **Masturbation Aid.** "The combination of porn and masturbation is good for anxiety reduction – a familiar safe vehicle for pleasure."

    "It's an outlet for sexual arousal, an outlet for helping to fall asleep easily."

[Note how easy it is to equate porn with masturbation, attributing to porn what are clearly the physical results of masturbation.]

10. **Expanding Sexual Imagination.** "It definitely added to my repertoire of sexual activity, teaching me about things I can do and expanding my imagination sexually. Like the *Kama Sutra*, *The Joy of Sex*, or others books of that ilk, porn can offer some really solid education in the sexual arts."

   "Because I really use hook-up sites rather than videos, that format of 'porn' has created an opportunity to explore some of the edgier things I might not have explored otherwise. If I were in a bar facing a potential sex partner for the first time, I might not own up to certain desires. The mask of the screen name has enabled me to gauge receptiveness before committing to a meeting."

   "It's a way to explore what else is out there in terms of sexual interests."

   "It has also provided a window into what other gay men do in terms of sex. This is particularly true of today's porn on the Internet which is done by amateurs or regular people who like to post what they do on the Internet but not true of traditional or 'professional' porn which is a more idealized version of what people may do."

11. **Broaden the Experience of What's Attractive.** "The biggest positive effect (gay) porn has had on me was to help me be interested in a wider range of types. It was really striking to me several times to see some guy I thought was hot, and then realize that he had some physical trait that I thought was bad in me, but it looked good in him. Back in high school and maybe 10-20 years after that, my idea was a male was supposed to have narrow hips and broad shoulders. Since I don't, those contributed

to my ugliness in my eyes. Now, thanks in part to porn, I find curves on guys very exciting. I love big butts, and though broad shoulders are very nice, so are not-so-broad shoulders. Porn has helped me that way with my opinions of a number of physical traits. I used to think a guy should definitely have a big dick, and that my average size was a terrible character flaw, but it's not a big deal to me now. Porn helped an enormous amount with this, by showing me all kinds of really hot guys who didn't have huge dicks."

12. **Gives Permission to Look.** "I've used gay porn deliberately to condition myself to like and feel comfortable with dicks and buttholes. They were definitely items of interest for me before porn, but I had trouble really looking at them. Only recently have I not felt mildly repulsed by them when I wasn't horny."

13. **Positive Conditioning.** "I have consciously used porn to condition myself to oral sex. I positively disliked guys' sucking my dick and just said no to some of them, never let anyone suck me off, never sucked anyone's dick and didn't want to. Seeing it about forty million times on videos, sometimes making myself watch it, showed me it could feel good to have my dick sucked, and at least could feel like an achievement to suffer through the boredom and cheek muscle discomfort of sucking someone off. One of my most exciting sexual experiences, after that, was the time I deep-throated a guy with a long dick. It really wasn't so sexual, but it was very intense physically, with the gagging, discovering that I produced copious saliva, and feeling something move of its own accord in my throat."

"It helps me open up to my sexual inhibitions. Inspires me to work on myself sexually. Be more comfortable and open with my partner."

14. **Maintains Libido.** "At times of stress, porn keeps me interested in sex."

    "I have a very intense routine. Porn helps me keep my libido."

    "Watching porn keeps a general buzz of erotic/sensual energy in me. Since my work in tantra I usually watch, masturbate, but I do not come. I find building energy and containing it without release gives me even more energy and attention in my daily life."

15. **Energy Release.** "Jerking off to porn is a wonderful way of releasing energy I find that builds in my body. Oddly, yoga and Qigong do similar things but they aren't as much fun."

16. **Generates Liberating Fantasies.** "Fantasies can be freeing, if one doesn't obsess."

    "Porn has been a good place to take my fantasies and act them out."

17. **Widen Network of Social/Sexual Contacts.** "In the category of social media as real-life porn, I'd say I've befriended a range of interesting men whom I might not have met in my usual circle. It's pretty clear I could only have met them through promiscuous sex. This makes me regret the pigeonholing I sometimes did in my youth, when I kept life and sex more separate."

18. **Sex Tips.** "I have learned some dialogue."

    "I discovered the beauty of edging, my new guilty pleasure."

"Porn has taught me techniques and introduced new fetishes (for lack of a better word) into my sexual vocabulary."

"I genuinely watch for new techniques and positions, which sounds a little like reading *Playboy* for the articles. I think I've gotten some sexual confidence from watching porn. I pick up 'styles' of being, ways of interacting sexually. I think it's helped me in learning how to be a top."

19. **Encouragement of Expression.** "I am more extroverted, no suppression."

20. **Promotes Staying in Shape.** "Porn drives me to keep up physical activity to maintain fit shape."

    "I would say that it makes me a little more inclined to get to the gym."

21. **Expands One's Image Library.** "It adds to the image repertoire—it's part of the overall stream of imagery that enters into and enriches my psychic life."

    "It allows me to see unconditional physical 'worship' of all body parts."

22. **Intensifies Erotic States.** "Porn provides a pathway into a highly concentrated erotic state, a fugue state perhaps. Joe Kramer talks about the way the access to a vast diversity of porn makes it possible for individuals to focus on precisely those images that will take them to the highest possible state of arousal."

23. **Provides Safe Outlet.** "Porn has kept me out of bars/boothstores looking for potentially dangerous situations and risky behavior."

24. **Early Education.** "Porn provided an avenue for exploration of what I was into when opportunities for sexual exploration were severely limited, back at school. Also it was a way to satisfy a deep hunger to see men naked when it was tough to get that in real life. As such, it was an opportunity to revel in the pleasures of a newfound sexual identity."

25. **Preparation for Real-Life Encounters.** "In rare instances, well-written porn taking a 'my first time' angle did in fact give me some reasonable ideas of what to expect when first experiencing things myself."

26. **A Step on the Road to Coming Out.** "The act of buying porn was an early step toward coming out: it was the first thing I ever did in a semi-public context that demonstrated that I was not some random straight guy."

27. **Entertainment.** "Sometimes I used it for the pure entertainment value of it."

    "It has provided a lot of entertainment."

28. **Promotes Romantic Fantasies.** "Because of my preference for material that depicts men connecting naturalistically (unscripted) and affectionately in text, photos or videos, it helps maintain a fantasy for me that some men can make those satisfying connections, that they can celebrate each other, and it keeps a candle of hope burning that there may be someone out there with whom I could establish a continuing relationship with a celebratory, erotic element."

29. **Gives Pleasure.** "It gives me pleasure, something I often deny myself."

30. **Increases Respect for Diversity.** "Porn has positively impacted my life in that I respect that our community is composed of many different people who get off in a variety of ways. Although, I am not personally interested in leather, I relish that others do get off on it. There is something for all of us and I respect all of it."

31. **A Fun Way to Celebrate Difference in a Relationship.** "Sometimes I'll share pictures that turn me on with my partner, even though he has different visual targets and appetites as far as porn is concerned."

BIBLIOGRAPHY

Books

Dangerous Bedfellows Collective. *Policing Public Sex* (South End Press, 1996).

Delany, Samuel. *Times Square Red, Times Square Blue* (New York University Press, 1999).

Dines, Gail. Pornland: *How Porn Has Hijacked Our Sexuality* (Beacon Press, 2010).

Downs, Alan. *The Velvet Rage* (Da Capo Press, 2005).

Freud, Anna. *The Ego and the Mechanisms of Defense* (International Universities Press, 1938).

Gooch, Brad. *The Golden Age of Promiscuity* (Alfred A. Knopf, 1996).

Herdt, Gilbert. *Ritualized Homosexuality in Melanesia* (University of California Press, 1984).

Hillman, James. *The Force of Character: And the Lasting Life* (PenguinRandomHouse, 1999).

Maier, Thomas. *Masters of Sex: The Life and Times of William Masters and Virginia Johnson* (Basic Books, 2009).

Moore, Thomas. *The Re-Enchantment of Everyday Life* (Harper Collins, 1996).

Morin, Jack. *The Erotic Mind* (Harper Collins, 1995).

Nitschke, Gunther. T*he Silent Orgasm* (Taschen, 1995).

Preciado, Paul. *Testo Junkie* (The Feminist Press, 2013).

Preston, John. *My Life as a Pornographer* (Masquerade Books, 1993).

Ramer, Andrew. *Two Flutes Playing* (Alamo Square Press, 1997).

Spanbauer, Tom. *The Man Who Fell in Love with the Moon* (Grove Press, 1991).

Tom of Finland, *retrospective* (Tom of Finland Foundation, 1988).

Articles

Boffey, Philip. http://www.nytimes.com/1982/08/24/science/skinner-tells-colleagues-his-personal-strategies-for-managing-old-age.html

Califia, Pat, "The New Puritans," *The Advocate*, April 17, 1980

—"The Great Kiddy Porn Sacre of '778 and Its Aftermath," *The Advocate*, October 16, 1980.

Christgau, Robert. "Pornography as Ideology and Other Ways to Get Off," *Village Voice*, July 15-21, 1981.

Doughtery, Conor. "Growing Up Mobile," *New York Times*, January 3, 2016.

Fledermaus (Tony DeBlase). "CBT: Cock & Ball Torture," *DungeonMaster #45*, undated.

Fremont-Smith, Eliot. "Pornography's Progress," *Village Voice*, October 15-21, 1980.

Goldstein, Richard. "Pornography and Its Discontents," *Village Voice*, October 16, 1984.

Holleran, Andrew. "Notes on Porn," *Gay and Lesbian Review*, Sept-Oct 2015.

Hollibaugh, Amber. "The Erotophobic Voice of Women," *New York Native*, September 26-October 9, 1983.

Kerner, Ian. "The Case for Porn," *Psychotherapy Networker*, Jan-Feb 2016.

Ley, David J. "Your Brain on Porn – it's NOT addictive," *Psychology Today*. https://www.psychologytoday.com/blog/women-who-stray/201307/your-brain-porn-its-not-addictive

Moylan, Brian. "How to Quit Porn and Not Entirely Ruin Your Life," *VICE*. https://www.vice.com/en_us/article/5gw4j3/how-to-quit-porn-and-not-entirely-ruin-your-life

Segal, David. "Does Porn Hurt Kids?" https://www.nytimes.com/2014/03/29/sunday-review/does-porn-hurt-children.html

Shewey, Don. "Daddy/Boy"

"Getting to the Bottom of It," *Gay.com*, October 1, 2010.

"The Gift of Desire," *Edge Online*, May 19, 2013.

"What's Hot About Porn?" *Edge Online*, September 19, 2013.

"Rose and Thorn: Notes on Porn," *Re/Porn: a zine about fag porn*, Abundant Fuck Books, 1977; reprinted online at Nightcharm.com.

"The Secret Life of Wally Shawn," *Esquire*, October 1983.

"Sexual Healing: Joseph Kramer Sings the Body Electric," *Village Voice*, April 21, 1992.

"Tony Kushner's Sexy Ethics," *Village Voice*, April 20, 1993.

Sommers-Flanagan, John. "Entering the danger zone," *Counseling Today*, November 2014.

Willis, Ellen. Column, *Village Voice*, October 15, 1979.

— Column, *Village Voice*, November 12, 1979.

— "Nature's Revenge" (review of Susan Griffin's *Pornography and Silence*), *New York Times Book Review*, July 12, 1981.

Film/Video

Alber, Matt. "Handsome Man" (2014).

Bailey, Fenton, and Randy Barbato, P*ornography: the secret history of civilization*, BBC-TV series.

DaSilva, Antonio. *Spunk* (2015).

Lewin, Ben. *The Sessions* (2012).

Kramer, Joseph. *Porn Yoga* (2015).

Nolot, Jacques. *Porn Theater* (2003).

Perel, Esther. "The secret to desire in a long relationship," TED Talk (2013).

Themi, Dr. Tim, "Sex, Porn, and Morality" (2014).

Wilson, Gary. "The Great Porn Experiment," TED Talk (2012).

ACKNOWLEDGMENTS

I am most indebted to the hundreds of men I've worked with for the last 20 years as a therapist, sacred intimate, teacher, and workshop facilitator. Their willingness to share with me their sexual histories, their struggles, their triumphs, and their quest for healing has inspired me and challenged me to think, listen, read, and understand more deeply and compassionately about the material that emerged in the writing of this book. I'm eternally grateful to the teachers who helped me develop a skillful practice, including Joseph Kramer, Collin Brown, Chester Mainard, Patricia Tucker, Ron DeAngelo, Sylvia Rosenfeld, and Alan Cohen. I learned a lot from conducting classes and retreats with my treasured colleagues John Ballew and Kai Ehrhardt.

Numerous people provided specific concrete support for the writing of this book. Keith Hennessy has been my soul brother since we met in 1991, when his queer pagan anarchist charisma fueled the Body Electric School's revolutionary sacred intimate training. In 1997 Keith published "Re/Porn: a zine about fag porn," for which he commissioned from me an essay that contained the seeds of this book. (That essay was reprinted online by Frederick Woodruff on the pioneering website Nightcharm.com.) Our conversations over the years have widened my perspective on sexuality, masculinity, and pornography. Keith helped recruit participants in my Use of Porn Study (as did Roger Gindi and Jeff Vilensky), and I want to thank the 50 men from all over the US and abroad who responded to that survey; their data and reflections influenced the formulation of my perceptions in many ways.

Keith Hennessy also read and gave valuable notes

on the manuscript at a crucial stage of the writing, as did Steve Schwartzberg, David Kurnick, and Wayne Hoffman. Wayne and his husband Mark Sullivan gave me the use of their house for a very helpful writing retreat, as did Robert Johansen; I appreciate their hospitality and generosity. Michael Bronski, an old friend from Boston gay liberation days, did me the enormous favor of reading the finished manuscript, offering notes, and advising me extensively on the minutiae of publishing this book. I gratefully accepted the seasoned counsel of Mitchell Waters at Curtis Brown Agency. Killian Malloy took several chunks I composed as blog posts and published them as online articles for Edge Media Network. I'm thrilled that the great Chip Kidd was willing to design the book jacket, and I feel fortunate that ace designer Todd Cooper agreed to give the interior pages a stylish look.

David Enn went above and beyond the call of duty as a friend, not only closely reading two vastly different drafts of the book and sharing extremely focused notes but repeatedly inquiring about my progress and supplying unstinting encouragement and passionate engagement with the material. Michael Cohen and Glenn Berger heard about and championed this project every step of the way. Other friends and colleagues have supported me and my life in ways that directly fed this book: Marta Helliesen, Tim Cooley, Harvey Redding, Adam Baran, Kirk Read, Gil Kessler, David Zinn, Ben Seaman, Paul Pinkman, Michael Mele, and Andy Holtzman.

Everything in my life benefits from daily infusions of physical joy, intellectual companionship, tech support, laughter, and love from my husband, Andrew Willett.

ABOUT THE AUTHOR

Don Shewey is a writer, therapist, and pleasure activist in New York City. As a journalist and critic, he has published three books about theater and written hundreds of articles for *the New York Times, the Village Voice, Esquire, Rolling Stone*, and other publications. He has chronicled his psycho-sexual-spiritual adventures in essays that have been included in numerous anthologies, including *The Politics of Manhood, Best of the Best Gay Erotica, The Queerest Art: Essays on Gay and Lesbian Theater,* and *Men Like Us: the GMHC Guide to Gay Men's Sexual, Physical, and Emotional Well-Being*. He is a New York state-licensed psychotherapist whose private practice specializes in sex and intimacy coaching. His work as a teacher and community health activist revolves around healing through pleasure, adult sex education, and grounded daily spiritual practice. He is active on social media and maintains two blogs, Another Eye Opens (cultural commentary) and Food for the Joybody (smart thinking about sex, intimacy, and life in a body). An archive of his writing is available online at donshewey.com.

www.ingramcontent.com/pod-product-compliance
Lightning Source LLC
Chambersburg PA
CBHW052023070526
44584CB00016B/1874